ALICE CONNER

Remnants from the Attic in My Mind

High Shoes and Bloomers

outskirtspress
DENVER, COLORADO

High Shoes and Bloomers
Remnants from the Attic in My Mind

v2.0

Cover image by Fred F. Selfridge, Jr.

Outskirts Press, Inc.
http://www.outskirtspress.com

ISBN: 978-1-4787-2071-3

PRINTED IN THE UNITED STATES OF AMERICA

Table of Contents

ACKNOWLEDGMENTS i
NOTE TO THE READERS iii
FOREWORD iv
PROLOGUE vi

PART I—MEET THE CONNER CLAN

CHARLES ALLISON (MICKEY) CONNER 1
MAGGIE MCKENZIE MILTON CONNER 7
FROM ISABELLA TO ALICE 15
SIBLING DYNAMICS 17
#1 MARGARET ANN…THE CHIEF 19
#2 RUTH EVELYN…THE QUIET ONE 23
#3 ETHEL LOUISE…THE SEAMSTRESS 25
#4 CHARLOTTE ALLISON…THE FEISTY ONE 28
#5 STANLEY BENJAMIN…THE CLOWN "PAT" 31
#6 LAWRENCE HARLOW …THE GREAT DEBATER "LARRY" 33
#7 HELEN MAY…THE GARBAGE COLLECTOR 36
#8 JEAN ELIZABETH…THE CLOTHES HORSE 38
#9 HENRY JAMES…MR CLEAN "JIM" 41
#10 CHARLES ALLISON JR. … THE (milk) PITCHER ("CHUCK") 44
#11 ALLY ARRIVES 47

PART II—OUR HOUSE IN THE HARBOR

THE BIG BLACK STOVE 50
UPSTAIRS…THREE BEDROOMS, MANY KIDS 52

THE GIRLS' ROOM....54
PEE-UP-ME-BACK-ALLY....56
DOUBLE BED, DOUBLE TROUBLE....59
THE GRATE IN THE BEDROOM FLOOR....61
JOEY AND I....65
THE BIG BOX....67
ONE SIZE LARGER, PLEASE....69
SIDE BY SIDE....71
INSTILLING THE WORK ETHIC....75
THE ABOMINABLE CELLAR....80
THE WOODSHED AND BEYOND....85
HIGH SHOES AND BLOOMERS....88
MUSICAL MOUSETRAP....90
MOM'S HANDS....95
PENNED PLAYMATES....99

PART III—GROWING UP IN THE HARBOR

THE HARBOR....104
TRAIN TRACKS....108
SUMMER SHENANIGANS....112
UNEXPECTED SUMMER EXCITEMENT....116
WINTER IN THE HARBOR....121
SEX ED… LEARNED, NOT TAUGHT....127
ALLY'S MUSICAL DEBUT....133
FOOD FOR THE TAKING?....135
DASTARDLY DEEDS....139
PEARL HARBOR DAY....142
OUR VOLUNTEER FIRE DEPARTMENT....145
CLAMBAKES....148
MY FATHER, THE END MAN....150
MAGGIE'S LEGACY, HOME COOKIN'....152
EPILOGUE....157
ABOUT THE AUTHOR....160

ACKNOWLEDGMENTS

One person may have written this book, but it took many more than that for it to come to fruition.

Many thanks to Doug Cooper, my editor and mentor…an author in his own right of the wonderful memoir, *Ting and I*. Doug is a remarkable man who guided me through the maze of organizing a book. His constructive criticism was instrumental in helping me to create a book that is more readable and to realize my potential as a writer.

The staff at the Montgomery [NY] Free Library is an exceptional group. They, more than once, dropped everything to find the resource books I needed when I needed them, and went out of their way to help me in other areas. I thank them for their support and enthusiasm.

My thanks go to my siblings, Charlotte, Helen, Jean, Jim, and Chuck, for their time and indulgence while fielding my frequent phone calls, and for searching back in their memories for me. My memories were in the "attic of my mind" but they were able to help me brush away cobwebs that were obscuring some of the details.

Judy Axtell and Jean Sutter, working as a team, spent untold hours listening to, reading, and proofreading this book. I thank them for their perseverance, endurance, and support during this whole publication process. They have earned an all-expenses-paid week in Aruba. Unfortunately, they will have to settle for a full-course dinner at my home in Montgomery. Better friends cannot be found. Thank you, Jean and Judy.

Many thanks I send to my friend Connie Derrenbacker, who, with her enthusiasm, was the first to convince me that this book would be interesting, entertaining, and worth publishing. Also, to my grandson-in-law, Joshua Klein, for making sure that the pages, while being written, were properly stored so that they couldn't get "lost in cyberspace." I thank my granddaughter, Angie Selfridge, who guided me, a novice, through troublesome moments in dealing with the computer. Special thanks to my #2 son, Fred Jr., (Skip) for lending his talent in designing the cover for my book.

I express my gratitude to my sons, Larry, Skip, Rick, and Andy, who have always believed in and supported me. They have had the "You can do it, Mom" attitude regarding any project I have tackled. This project has been no different. It is hard to slack off when others have such faith.

My thanks go to my daughters-in-law, Gail and Sue, who are both experts in family cooking, and have become like the daughters I never had. Also, I cherish the memory of my late daughters-in-law, Vicky and Laurie, who through illnesses were taken from us far too soon.

Last but not least, I acknowledge with thanks and love my fan club--- my grandchildren: Eric, Ally, Lanny, Sadie, Chris, Angie, Kasey, and Lowell, all of whom brighten my kitchen, and my day, when they come through the door… one at a time or as a group. Without you, this book would have had no purpose. The legacy is in your hands. Instill it tenderly. Pass it on steadfastly. Teach my great-grandchildren the value of family and love.

NOTE TO THE READERS

Periodically, in this book, you will find words that you may question as "legitimate," and/or that do not appear in your dictionary. I call these "Alicisms." Sometimes there is no "adult" word to describe what a child is seeing (or thinking), and so I revert, of necessity, to the child in me and create a word that fits...just as children do (until they are repeatedly corrected and give up this practice).

For my siblings who might be reading this, if your memory of any of the following stories is different than mine, that is understandable. Just as we can all look at a painting and see it differently, all, (or at least most) of us will remember events differently. Please allow that what I have written about my growing-up years has been drawn from my memory bank, since I did not have the key to yours.

Since you are all older than I, your memories have had more time to mellow, grow, shrink, or become cloudier or more exaggerated. If you feel you must take issue with any of the stories, please don't tell me...just sit down and write a book based on your memories. I promise I will read it.

All of us have, somewhere, a child within us that we choose to ignore or stifle for fear that he will embarrass us (should he be allowed to surface). As an adult reading this book, I ask one thing of you...please let the child come out! Walk with me-like two children together-into the abominable cellar, balance on the tracks over the trestle, catch the peppermint patty, and taste the cold sweetness of a spoonful of ice cream on a hot night. Let yourself go and, come, with me.

Be a child again, just for a while.

Alice Conner Selfridge, Author

FOREWORD

No dust clings to the items from Alice Conner Selfridge's mental attic. Her bright stories from the years 1933-1945, which included the Depression and World War II, put you amid a family of 13, eking out a living on a family farm in northern Massachusetts, in Townsend Harbor, where there were no ships and the population was a few hundred.

During much of this period, Alice's father, Mickey Conner, earned around $7 a week at the factory across the street. Her mother, Maggie, a city girl displaced to a country farm, eventually had 11 children (really 12, counting Isabella, who died three days after she was born).

"We didn't know we were poor," Alice writes. This book tells of Ally's first twelve years, generally very pleasant years, on that big-family farm. The stories are almost all happy ones.

She started out as "Pee-Up-Me-Back Ally," youngest of the brood, and was teased when young for her small size and her pigeon-toed walk. Not knowing the rest of the clan, I would still guess her parents had "saved the best for last." This warm, captivating memoir tells of a childhood that was fun and hard work, and the almost-eighty Alice Selfridge who let me edit her book, projects in person a sturdy, good-humored intelligence contained in a wiry physique and graced with a ready smile---a woman who made our weekly meetings enjoyable and productive.

Why did she admire both her mother and her father, two very different people? How did they feed and clothe such a crew?

What happened when the cat was put in the barrel with the rat?

What happened when her father struck the barrel with a sledgehammer? What was in the "big box" and what was creepy about the cellar? How close did Ally come to drowning in the pond? Scores of vignettes and profiles illuminate life in the Conners' not-so-little house by the leatherboard factory and the Harbor Pond.

You will enjoy reading Ally's memoir about her early years. A second work about her later life may well follow this one.

Douglas Winslow Cooper, Ph.D.
Walden, NY 12586
douglas@tingandi.com
21 June 2012

PROLOGUE

Late Night Thoughts From The Attic of My Mind

I guess it must be time to tell my story. I wake up in the middle of the night and the sentences and paragraphs are running through my head, keeping me from going back to sleep. It almost seems as though I have a jigsaw puzzle of words and they tumble around in my head until I take the time to set them into a pattern that makes a picture for others to read.

I am not sure why, after all this time of "piddling with poetry" that the story seems important. I mean, usually it's rhymes that keep me awake, going around and around in my brain until I get up and write them down. This time it's the story.

Maybe I am starting to realize my age and I have, somewhere in my subconscious, begun to think that if I don't start it soon, I may be finished before it is. Not that I am planning on dying very soon, but I know how slow I am in getting facts down, and I would like to get all the facts on paper, as I remember them.

Now, if you're starting to read this, thinking you are going to be treated to some wonderfully exciting story, you had best put it down and go to the nearest library or bookstore, because this is a story about the early years of my life. Those years were not boring, for sure. They were hard years and fun years, all mixed in together. But then, being a child in a large family in the 1930s and 1940s was both… hard and fun.

This story is not being written primarily for the general public, but more for my grandchildren. I would like them to know who their Lil'

Nana was. I need to write it down for several reasons. I like to organize things that I know will stay organized. Writing is organizing thoughts and is quite unlike organizing my drawers or closets that become a big jumble again in a day or a week after I have set them right. Like my underwear drawer. I gave up on that a long time ago! All those silky, slippery things that, as soon as they are neatly stacked, start falling over and slipping in different directions and soon end up in a jumble again, waiting to be organized once more.

When I think about it, life is kind of like that --- just when I think it's the way I want it, something happens to jumble it up and I have to sort it out and get it back in order. I think that if I put it down on paper though, after the fact, at least that part will stay organized. Then I can go back and look at it again and again, and it will still be the same. It will no longer be a hodgepodge of happenings and events scattered helter-skelter in my brain with the events I am presently trying to recall, hiding in the deepest depths, refusing to surface.

Rather like the bra that I was trying to find to wear today.

Yes, it is time to tell my story.

PART I
MEET THE CONNER CLAN

We didn't know we were poor
Ally, Mom, Chuck, Jim, Jean, Helen

1936, Mickey and Ethel

Maggie Conner, 1936

Mickey and Maggie

Mickey coming home from work

Pansy stand
House in the harbor

Joey and Ally, early 1940s

Pat and Larry, 1940s

Front: Jim, Charlotte, Ally, Helen
Back: Margaret, Larry, Ruth, Chuck, Ethel, Jean

CHARLES ALLISON (MICKEY) CONNER

I think that it's important before I go any further, to introduce you to the two people responsible for my being. I also want to tell you a little bit about them, although you will find bits and pieces of their lives and personalities scattered throughout my stories.

Mickey, (I never heard anyone call him "Charles," "Charlie," or "Chuck;" and my mother used to call him "Al"), was born somewhere near Boston on June 21, 1884, and passed away in October, 1962. He married Maggie McKenzie Milton, and together they had a total of 12 children, all of whom you will read about in the following pages.

Mickey was a man who was small in stature, but loud in voice and hot in temper. I have never been totally sure just how tall he was, but I don't think he stood much over 5'5". I have pictures of him and others standing side by side, and that is the best "guesstimate" I can make as to his height. He may have weighed 130 lbs. at his heaviest, but I seriously doubt it. He was short, slim, very wiry and, if I remember correctly, very strong!

At this point, I have had to piece together what I could in regards to Mickey's early life. I think that either he didn't talk much about his childhood or else by the time the twelfth kid came along, he was tired of telling the same stories over and over, so didn't tell any to me. The information I have is mostly from pictures and from stories my *elder* sisters have told me. I am not sure if some of this information is accurate, nearly accurate, or pure fiction, but I am passing it on anyway.

The one thing that I am positively sure of is that Mickey was a proud, hard-working man, a strong believer in the work ethic, and a man who dearly loved his wife and children. He, unfortunately, never learned how to express his love verbally, and that led us, as young children, to believe that he did not, in fact, love us. At least, that was my perception until I was much, much older.

I can remember, as a very young child, being quite afraid of him, and yet, being thrilled when he would ask (no, tell) me to sit on the end of a long piece of wood that he had set across two sawhorses, to anchor one end down as he cut the other end. It's pretty funny to me now, because I probably didn't weigh more than 40 lbs., if that. I must have been a pretty lightweight anchor… apparently heavy enough to suit his purpose, though. It also seems funny to me now that I would have been so happy to just sit on a piece of wood while he sawed, but, in retrospect, I think it was getting his attention that probably thrilled me.

Mickey would, occasionally, call upon me to sing a song when we had company. I would be so happy and proud that my father wanted me to sing. I don't remember his asking my sisters and brothers to sing, but I imagine he did before I was born. Either that, or I was the hammy one from birth, and he knew it!

Mickey was the oldest of five children born to Stanley J. Conner and Sophia Nickerson Conner. He grew up, as I understand, in a not-so-nice area of the Boston suburbs. His father was a carpenter who was reportedly involved in the building of many of the tenement homes around Boston. I have been told (I am not sure by whom) that Mickey only went as far as fifth or sixth grade in school. He left school to go to work with his father, doing carpentry.

It was not unusual, in those days, for children to quit school at an early age and go to work. This was usually of necessity and sanctioned by the parents. That would have been around 1895, and life was very hard in those days. By that time, there would have been five children, the youngest just having been born, and it was very difficult to feed that many children. When they got old enough to go out and work, they assisted by bringing money in to support the household. At least, the older boys did.

I know none of the specifics about how my parents met. They were married in late 1912 or early 1913. Mickey was a carpenter and also drove a trolley car (he called them "streetcars") in and around the greater Boston area. He was also, at one time or another, a fireman and a policeman, but I have no knowledge of whether these were volunteer or paying positions. I have a couple of pictures of him in uniforms, so I do know he worked in some capacity for these departments. What other jobs he held to keep his growing family fed, I am not sure. He was always working. His family, while poor, did have the necessities of life.

Mickey and Maggie had their first five children while they lived in and around the city of Boston. Sometime around 1921-22, they packed up their belongings and their children and moved to Townsend Harbor, where Mickey got a job in a factory and proceeded to learn how to farm and raise his own animals and food to supplement what his meager income could buy. He also worked doing carpentry for various people in town.

This was no small undertaking for a man who had grown up in the Boston suburbs, and, I assume, had little or no knowledge of how to grow vegetables. His family was still growing. While many families were on welfare and/or receiving some kind of public assistance, Mickey refused any help. When I was growing up we lived in the duplex across the street from the factory where my father worked. I remember one morning in summer he came rushing in the backdoor and questioned my mother as to where the "welfare" man was. My mother answered that the truck was parked out front, but the man had gone into the house next door (the other side of our large duplex home). My father then reiterated that he did not want to see him at our house. "I can take care of my own without any help from Welfare," he stated. As I said, he was a proud man.

After moving to Townsend Harbor, Mickey also became involved in the community. He was an active member of the fire department and, I believe at one time, the police force, and was involved in many activities in the town, such as minstrel shows, etc. (Some of these community activities will be further explained later on). I don't know when he found the time. He would be at work at 7 a.m. and work until 4 p.m. In the summer months after work, he would work in the gardens, sometimes until dark and/or go to work on a carpentry project for some neighbor. He was not alone in this struggle for survival. He was married to a lady (Maggie) who worked just as hard as he did. Maggie is another chapter.

Mickey had a hot temper. When he blew, no one argued. It was hard to know what might set him off. I know I never dared to do anything but try to disappear when he lost his temper.

I remember one time, when I was around 11 or 12, and he came down to breakfast. My mom had fixed his usual fried egg for him. Mickey liked his eggs cooked so hard that they resembled those plastic fried eggs that you see in a joke shop. There could not be the slightest trickle of yolk. Well, she had made him a fried egg sandwich that morning, and when he bit into it, there was a small trickle of yolk. Mickey picked up the plate, with the sandwich on it, and threw it against the kitchen wall, where, of course, it splattered the egg, and broke the dish to smithereens.

My mother never said a word. My father just got up from the table, grabbed his jacket, and walked out of the house to go to work. After he left, Mom quietly picked up the pieces of the broken dish, picked up the egg and bread, and then got a cloth to clean the wall and the floor. I remember being upset with her for allowing him to "get away" with that behavior and encouraged her to just leave the mess there until he cleaned it up himself... but that was not her way. My mother would do anything to avoid a confrontation and would just wait until he got over his anger.

It is true that Mickey had a short fuse. He appeared, at least to his family much of the time, to be a tyrannical man whose way you kept out of - especially if you had done something you were not supposed to do.

The other side of Mickey was the charming, laughing man who seldom seemed to get angry at all. This was the side seen by his friends and acquaintances. My mom used to call him "home devil, street angel," and I think that was an apt description. I never saw him express any type of anger, or even be upset, when we had company or when he was out with others.

Everybody loved Mickey. Of course, it is no wonder that everyone loved him. He was quick to invite anyone to stay for dinner or spend the night at our house... in spite of the fact that there wasn't an empty bed available, since they were all filled with kids. However, it was not a surprise to us to occasionally come downstairs on a Sunday morning and find someone sleeping on the floor in the living room, or on the living room couch. This did not happen frequently, but it did happen often enough to remain in my memory.

The other soft side of Mickey was seen at affairs such as weddings, graduations, and funerals. He spent much of his time convincing us that he was a hard-hearted man, but he had his <u>very</u> soft moments. He expressed his love and caring in unexpected ways that we were only able to understand and appreciate when we were older. I saw his soft side at my high school graduation when he bought me roses, and again on my wedding day, when the minister asked, "Who gives this woman in marriage?" My father was crying so hard (as he, unknowingly, stood on my train,) that he had a difficult time saying, "I do" in answer to the question. I will talk about some of his other soft moments in upcoming pages.

In retrospect, my father, (I called him Papa) did the best he knew how with what he had. I am not sure how even-tempered and tolerant I would be if I had eleven kids to support. If I had eleven kids, I would be spending all my time checking on them to be sure they were growing up right and doing the right things. Mickey didn't have time to check on us all the time, so I think his strategy was to parent with a hard hand, and a no-questions-asked attitude. Then, with a few scare tactics thrown in, no one would *dare* get into trouble!

Of course, this didn't always work with all of us, but for the most part, we knew that if we got into trouble with teachers, policemen or neighbors, the consequences were nothing compared to what they would be when our father found out. We did try to avoid any situations that might result in having to face "the wrath of Mickey."

MAGGIE MCKENZIE MILTON CONNER

I am still in the process of trying to find out where, exactly, my mom was born. I was told as a child that she was born in Kentucky and that may very well be, but it has, so far, been impossible to verify, because all records in the town in Kentucky where we think she was born, were destroyed by fire. I also have no idea how she and my grandparents came to live in Boston.

My mother was christened Maggie McKenzie Milton, a good Scottish name. She was proud of her heritage, as was her father. However, when she was a child in school, in the late 1800s, "Maggie" was not an accepted name in the United States, so her report card bore the name "Margaret." The first time she came home with her report card, before signing it, my grandfather wet his finger with saliva (spit) and rubbed out the "Margaret" and filled in the space with "Maggie." This, of course got my mother in trouble when she returned it to the teacher the next day. The teacher said she would have to sit in the "cold corner" as punishment. (Schoolrooms were heated with a wood/coal stove in those days, so the closer the stove, the warmer your seat.) I don't know if the issue was ever taken up directly with my grandfather or not.

I was told by Maggie that her mother died when she was very young (I have no idea of her age at that time) and that she was raised by my grandfather, Benjamin Milton. He was a baker and either owned his own bakery shop or worked in one. My mother did speak of going to the bakery in the early hours of the morning and helping to make baked goods, which were sold fresh to early-morning customers. I also know that she stayed with friends of my grandfather much of the time when she was growing up… possibly as a foster child or just a babysitting arrangement. I am not sure.

How do I describe Maggie? She had a patient, calm demeanor that I have never had (and probably never will.) That was one of the things I admired most about her. I always wished that I could emulate that part of her personality.

According to records I have obtained, Maggie was married to my father in 1921, when she was 21 years old, and had her first child in 1922. That child, a girl named Isabella May, only lived three days. I was told that my mother carried the tiny coffin to the cemetery on her lap. I am not sure who told me this, but it could well have been my mother when I was younger. Whether it is a fact or not, I cannot imagine the pain she must have gone through to lose a child at three days old. I was also told that my mother had diphtheria and somehow, I think the disease was connected to the baby's death but once again, I am not positive. It seems that my mom had probably contracted and recovered from the disease either just before she got pregnant with Isabella, or shortly after.

Maggie was a tiny woman in her younger years, probably not weighing much over 100 lbs., if in fact she weighed that much. She had small bones and I have pictures of her showing that she was as thin as I am (98 lbs.) until she approached 50. That's when she started to become heavier. Even though she stood only 5'2" or 5'3", she carried herself straight, and gave the illusion (to me at least) of being taller. She had a way about her that seemed to say "lady," even in a housedress and apron. I do not remember ever seeing my mother "drink" anything down in a manner that would indicate she was very thirsty. She always "sipped" at her drinks, whether it was tea, beer, or water, and I can remember wondering about this as a young child. Everyone else drank while Maggie sipped.

One year after her first baby was born, her second child was born. After that another child was born almost every year and a half to two years, until I was born. Consequently, when my parents moved from Woburn, near Boston, to Townsend Harbor, they had four children, the oldest being seven. I suspect my mother was in the early months of pregnancy with the next child when that move occurred.

After the family moved to Townsend Harbor, my father went to work in the leatherboard factory, which was within walking distance of their home. My mother continued to have babies, and was kept busy caring for them. She also raised extra money by baking and selling bread and pies, and selling eggs from the chickens we raised. Mom also helped in the garden all summer; hoeing, weeding, planting, and reaping as needed, and then canning and preserving enough vegetables and fruit from the garden to keep the family fed for the whole winter. Where she learned these skills, I have no idea, but I will say, she was damned good at them!

Mom also played the piano and played it well. She could not, as far as I know, read music, but played by ear. I was told (I wish I could remember by whom), that she, in her younger years, had played accompaniment for silent movies at a theater in or near Boston. It was never hard for me to believe, because, even when her hands were arthritic, she could bring out sounds on the piano that would make everyone want to gather around and sing.

I cannot remember ever hearing my mother yell, but maybe she figured Mickey did enough of that for both of them. I can remember seeing her disappointment and her hurt but never her anger. She may have worked out her anger in some of the same ways she worked out her fear or anxieties. She was such a stoic woman during goodbyes to each of my four brothers when they went off into the Army or Navy. It was during war times, so her fear must have been great. After they left, Mom would disappear to the upstairs bedrooms and clean, clean, clean! It was very hard to isolate yourself in our house with so many people, but when Maggie was hurting or sad, she found a way to isolate and work through her pain. In retrospect, she probably figured cleaning was the one thing she could do that no one would interrupt for fear of being put to work. I think of a poem that I wrote many years ago, when my own sons (I also had four) had moved away from home. They had not gone into the armed services though, so I know I did not experience the pain and fear that Maggie had. The times were very different, but my son's empty bedroom inspired me to write a poem.

Empty Space
In the corner, a soldier doll,
High school pennant, on the wall
"Playboy" neatly in its stall
He is gone, after all

Maggie bore 12 children in 20 years and raised 11 of them in times that were hard. She was a loving and caring mother… one who instinctively mothered, having grown up with no role model. She never had a job outside the home (other than taking care of grandchildren). There was no time to fit in any other work but that which she did in the home and garden. She said to me, more than once, that she " would never be able to get a job outside, because she didn't know how to do anything, except maybe wash dishes in a restaurant." *Oh Mom, if you only knew the talents and skills you had! There is not a woman in today's world that could accomplish in a week what you used to accomplish in a day.* Now, we run our vacuum sweepers, punch in the buttons for the dishwasher, turn on the washer, hit the thermostat for heat and the AC for cool, throw the clothes in the dryer and then, once they are dry, just fold them… no need, for the most part, for ironing, since nearly everything is "wash and wear." Many of us purchase food that is already prepared for us. Heat and eat is the name of the game. Even our salads can be bought, ready made, in a bag, ready to serve.

Mom had certain days that she did certain things every week, with little deviation in her schedule. On Monday, she would wash clothes. This was no simple "throw them in the washer and walk away and when you come back they are washed, rinsed and spun dry" routine. We did not have running water. We had a small pump at the kitchen sink and so for her to do a wash, she first had to pump buckets full of water, carry them to the stove, and heat the water. Then she would pull the washing machine (which I remember as a big round tub type thing on wheels with a 'wringer' attached to the top of the back) into the middle of the kitchen. Behind this washing machine, she would set a big washtub on a chair or a table and fill it with cold water for rinsing. Many gallons of water had to be pumped and carried to fill the tub. She would then put the soap and hot water (carrying it again from the stove) into the washing machine, fill it with dirty clothes, and then turn on the "agitator" (at least it was electric by the time I came along). The clothes would wash for however long she felt they needed. Once they were washed, she would take them out of the tub, one at a time, and feed them through the wringer (which looked like two rolling pins, one stacked on top of the other). They would go through the wringer, (which squeezed the soapy water out of them). They then came out the other side of the wringer, and dropped into the rinse water in the big tub. After they were swished (by hand) in the rinse water, she would then feed them through the wringer again and they would drop into the laundry basket. Wow!

This procedure repeated itself over and over. The white clothes would always be washed first, then the light colors followed by the dark colors. This involved many loads of clothes, for many, many kids… plus the sheets and towels. I am sure though, that it didn't seem as hard for her then as it had been before she got an electric washing machine. Before, she had to scrub the clothes on a washboard in the big washtub!

While the second load was being washed, she would carry the heavy basket of wet clothes out to the clothesline where she would hang each item… summer, winter, fall or spring. There were days when it would be so cold the clothes would be frozen on the line before she finished hanging a load. There were also many times when her hands got frostbitten from hanging wet clothes outside when it was below freezing. There was, however, no other way to dry them. I used to think it was kind of neat because at the end of the day, if the sun didn't warm things up enough, we would bring the clothes in and they would be frozen solid. You could actually stand the pants or shirts upright and they would stay there for a while until they started to thaw. Then they would have to be draped over a rack or chair or something near the stove to dry out. But, they smelled sooooo good!!! We would climb into bed at night with sheets that were dried out on the clothesline all day. There is no other smell in this world that is quite like the smell of fresh, air-dried sheets.

I think there were about six or eight lines on her clothesline poles and every one of them was filled each Monday. Of course, unlike today, we were made to keep our clothes clean enough to wear again, partly because we didn't have that many clothes and partly because Mom only did laundry once a week. If you, for example, wore your red shirt on Tuesday and got it dirty, it was not going to be clean and available for you to wear on Friday, unless you rinsed it out yourself. Laundry would not be done again until the following Monday! Also, our "school clothes" had to be changed after school and we would don our "play clothes." The good clothes were saved for school. As you can imagine, washing was nearly an all day affair.

Tuesday, Mom would spend a good part of the day ironing all the clothes she had washed on Monday. As I said, virtually nothing was "wash and wear" except, maybe socks and underwear, so everything had to be ironed or it was a wrinkled mess! Ironing dresses, shirts and pants for eight or ten people is no easy task, believe me! Ironing involved heating the irons on the stove, as we didn't have an electric iron. Each iron, and they were exactly that - made of cast iron- had a little clip type hole in the top. When an iron got hot enough, my mom would clip this wooden handle onto one of the irons and iron with it until it cooled down. She would then place that back on top of the stove, unclip the handle and clip it onto the next iron, and so on and so on. I remember three irons. The irons did not take all the wrinkles out easily, and because there was no steam iron, many items had to be "sprinkled" and rolled in a ball to dampen them before you could get the wrinkles out.

I think Wednesday was a cleaning day, but I'm not totally sure. One sister has recently told me that Wednesday was another baking day. That makes sense because there is no way that baked goods could have lasted from Saturday to Saturday. I do know Thursday was shopping day. This too, happened only once a week, and would take almost all of Thursday afternoon…just to do grocery shopping.

On Thursdays, Mom would do housework in the morning and then at one o'clock, she would take the bus and go to Fitchburg (about 10 miles away) and do grocery shopping for the week. Now, you will remember that all of our vegetables were grown and canned, and much of our meat was home raised (chickens and pigs), but she still had to shop for "staples." Each Thursday, she would come home on the four o'clock bus and walk from the corner (equivalent to about a block away) carrying two big (and I do mean big) shopping bags. They were full to the brim with coffee, tea, salt, sugar, maybe some meat (usually hamburger or some kinds of beef, and fish) soaps, peanut butter, and many other things that were needed that we didn't grow or raise. Her fingers would be red and swollen when she got home from the twine handles on the shopping bags. And, of course, as soon as she got home, she had to unpack and put away and then start supper for the family.

I don't remember clearly, but I think Friday was probably a heavy cleaning day because Saturday was mostly spent cooking and baking for the weekend. There were no days that she didn't work. In fact, Saturday baking really started on Friday night when she would make the bread dough, so it could rise overnight and be ready to be baked on Saturday. Beans also got baked on Saturday, as did pies and any other pastries she might make.

Sunday a day of rest? I don't think so! Sundays, our house was often full of relatives who came up from "the city" to enjoy the country and my mother's cooking. That was also a day when, frequently, older siblings would come "home" to visit and often stay for Sunday dinner. There was never a lack of people to feed on Sunday! A large part of Maggie's Sunday was spent cooking.

How she, along with her regular housework, ever made time to work in the garden hoeing and picking vegetables plus doing all of the canning, is mind-boggling to me. She was not afraid to, occasionally, cut the head off of a chicken (though this job usually fell to the men or boys) to prepare for dinner. During the holidays, she would pluck, clean, and sell chickens to the neighbors for their Thanksgiving or Christmas dinners.

My mom was an amazing woman!

FROM ISABELLA TO ALICE

I was the twelfth child born to Maggie McKenzie Conner and Charles Allison "Mickey" Conner. The first child, a girl, lived only a few days. Her name was Isabella. After that, Maggie and Mickey had four more girls: Margaret, Ruth, Ethel, and Charlotte, followed by two boys, Stanley ("Pat") and Lawrence ("Larry"). After Larry, two more girls were born and named Helen and Jean, followed by two more boys who were named Henry James ("Jim") and Charles, Jr. ("Chuck") and last of all, me. There used to be jokes that I didn't understand about how I was the "scrapings of the pot." I didn't understand that one until I was well into high school.

I remember one time, when I was around seven years old; I found a picture in a magazine. I loved the picture but didn't understand the caption under it. It was a picture of a large dog curled up with one very small puppy lying beside it, and the large dog had a rather sad look on its face. The caption was "The Last of the Litter." I brought it to my mom and asked her what that meant, and she explained to me that this was the last baby that the mother had.

Not long after that, when I was in school, the discussion for our second -grade class was about how many brothers and sisters each of us had. I stood up and proudly announced that I had 10 brothers and sisters and, eager to impress with my newfound knowledge, announced that I was the "last of the litter." I honestly do not remember Mrs. Smith's expression (I wish I could), but I do remember my mother's face, as well as my older siblings' expressions, when I announced at the dinner table that night that I had passed on this information to the class. My mother was visibly upset, and my brothers and sisters thought it was the funniest thing they had heard for a while. I did not understand either reaction. After all, I was her last baby… last but not least.

SIBLING DYNAMICS

I feel sorry for people who grew up without brothers or sisters. When I was young, I used to envy them, thinking how nice it would be to not have to share attention, or toys, or anything else with anyone. I thought it would be especially wonderful to not have older brothers and sisters to boss you around. The sisters were the worst at being bossy, in my opinion.

I know now that having siblings, especially older ones, is like owning a computer disc that carries the events from before the time you were born, up until the time when your own memory kicks in. You have the advantage of being able to call up information about your family in the times before you had even been thought of. The more older siblings you have, the more facts you have available. Of course, the more older siblings you have, the more variation of these facts is available also. I have found that where one stood in the family line altered ones view of certain things. Let me explain a little further.

My brother, Chuck, is 19 months older than I. My sister, Jean, is about seven years older than I, with Jim in between those two. Next to Jean in the line, is Helen, who is nine years older than I am. Now, if you interviewed each of these three people and asked them what the youngest member of the family was like, you would get three or four completely different descriptions. You might even wonder if they were talking about the same person.

Brother Chuck would probably tell you (as he has told me numerous times) that I spent all of my time crying and running to tell mom what he was doing, and that my main mission in life was to be a total pain in the rear to him in the early years. Jim would probably agree with him, since they were close in age and a large portion of their younger years was spent together.

Jean was the last girl born before I, so had held the status of the "baby girl" in the family until I came along. Jean would probably tell you that I only needed to look cute and sing a song to get my parents' attention. She might paint a picture of this wispy little blonde, singing and dancing around the house and winning approving pats on the head for her behavior.

Sister Helen, who is next up the line from Jean, would describe me as an adorable, sweet little girl. Helen describes my arrival into the family as like "getting a real live doll". Helen will relate no negativity at all in my personality or behavior as a youngster. I am not sure how accurate any of these memories are, but I do know that if you were able to interview each of the 10 older siblings, you would get ten different images of me.

Being a member of a large family is rather like being in a room of trick mirrors. Everywhere you look, you get a different image of yourself. I do have to say though, that sister Jean's image is, at least, partly correct in that I did get much positive reinforcement when I performed. My father and mother both encouraged me and I am sure that is a large part of the reason that, to this day, I enjoy performing in nearly any capacity. My father, especially, did not give praise easily and this was one of the few ways I found that I could get his approval.

I may have been young, but I wasn't stupid! I took advantage of it!

#1 MARGARET ANN... THE CHIEF

How do I describe Margaret? Margaret, the first healthy child born to our parents, arrived on July 17, 1914, exactly one year and two days after the first child, Isabella, was born. I imagine that first year must have been quite a scary time for my parents, having lost their first baby at just a few days old. They must have spent some sleepless nights worrying whether Margaret was breathing or not, but Margaret did survive. I think Margaret was born with such a strong inherent resolution to survive, that had she been inflicted with a life-threatening disease, she would have pulled through due to pure, (sometimes) bull-headed determination. That part of Marg's individuality stayed with her throughout the rest of her life.

This elder sister was one to be loved, admired, enjoyed, and feared. She was what today's society would call a "clean freak." She truly enjoyed cleaning house, ironing, polishing silver, and all that went with it. She definitely liked things neat and in order. And she did not like people messing up what she had put in order. In short, Margaret was a taskmaster.

Margaret was also a good cook, and loved parties. She loved to dance and sing (though like her father before her, she could not carry a tune), and was happy when in charge of planning and prepping food for a party. At my wedding, when I was 18, she was in charge of planning and preparing the buffet dinner that was served. The sisters all worked as a team with the actual preparation, but Marg was the CEO. She was also one of my (many) bridesmaids. And, of course, it all went off beautifully.

Margaret had two children, Joanne "Joey" and Milton, when she divorced their father, Hector and moved to Providence, R.I. There she found work as a waitress, working over the years in several hotels and restaurants. She was an excellent waitress who had the skill of remembering nearly every customer she had served, which encouraged them to come back again and again.

I have few memories as a child of Margaret since she was 19 years older than I. I do know that when her first child, Joanne was born, I was nearly two years old, and it wasn't too long after that that I remember feeling as though I had been replaced, in Margaret's eyes, by this new baby. That feeling was short-lived because as Joanne got older, Margaret once again became a mother figure to me, only I was not the baby sister as much as the playmate for her daughter. Of course, I quickly learned that if there was a problem, her daughter was going to be the favored one, not her sister. I think Margaret tried, but where Joanne was concerned, Margaret was not always fair. Besides, I was the older one and so it was assumed that I was smart enough not to get into trouble… WRONG!

Joanne and I were out sliding down a hill next to Margaret's house one wintry afternoon. There was a brook (frozen over) that ran between Margaret's home and the adjoining property, and the sliding hill was on the opposite side of the brook. This meant that to get to the top of the hill, we would cross the frozen brook, climb the hill and then slide down, cross the brook at the bottom, and end up in Margaret's yard. We were young, maybe four and six years old, or a little older.

Old enough to be out playing alone... and Margaret could easily check on us from her window.

We climbed to the top of the hill and began our descent down. I was in front, leading the way with Joanne only seconds behind me. We were moving pretty fast when we came to the brook which was seldom very deep, and seemed to be frozen solid...except for the one part that I happened to steer towards in order to cross. I heard the crunching of ice breaking and the front of my sled went into the brook, sinking down, about 6 inches into the icy water. Before I could even catch my breath from the shock of the cold blast, Joey was in the brook next to me.

I got off my sled and with icy cold water over my little boots; I tried to help her get off her sled and out of the water. I succeeded in doing this just as Margaret came out the door, yelling "What's the matter with you? Didn't you check that ice before you tried to cross it?" Of course, she had checked the ice herself before we were allowed to go sliding. She just didn't bother to check the part that we chose as a crossing point. She was really angry with me and made no bones about it! "Ally, you get home, right now!" she said as she picked up the screaming Joanne and carried her in the house to get changed and warmed. I did not argue... nobody argued with Margaret. I grabbed the rope of my sled and started trudging home in wet boots and snowsuit. It wasn't a long walk home, only past the firehouse, post-office and two other houses, but that day, it seemed like miles to me.

Of course I got home, feeling very bad that I had caused Joey to get wet in the brook, but to be honest, I felt worse for me! I was wet and cold; she was in a nice warm house probably having a nice warm bath. I told Mom my version of what happened, and of course, I got stripped and rubbed and warmed quickly beside the stove, and though my mother was pretty quiet and easy-going, this time she was MAD! I could tell. Oh, she didn't yell or storm around or anything, but I knew she was mad... and not at me.

I am sure Margaret got a talking to before the day was out because as soon as I got snuggled under blankets on the couch, close to the big old iron stove, I heard her say to someone in the kitchen, "Keep an eye on her, I'll be right back." And all I could think was, "Margaret's gonna get it now!" And I am sure she did!

I am not sure why that story came to my mind when thinking about Margaret. She was always good to me, and I had some very memorable and enjoyable times, when in later years, I spent a few weeks vacationing at her house in R.I. She made sure that we always had a few coins to go to the park and was very generous when it came to taking us to Narragansett Bay and other places. She took us to the beach and amusement parks. I have to, once again though, reiterate… she was a no-nonsense lady. Perhaps a female version of Mickey, in a way. She would give you "the shirt off her back" if you were in need. I both feared and admired her, and never questioned her orders. But boy…I sure did love her!

Margaret died in November, 1996 at the age of 82

#2 RUTH EVELYN... THE QUIET ONE

Ruth was the second child, and the second girl (really the third if I count Isabella, but from here on, I will only be counting from the surviving children). Ruth was born on April 17, 1916... just 21 months after Margaret.

Ruth was, to me, "the quiet one." She seemed to avoid the petty squabbles that other siblings became involved in, and would prefer to walk away rather than be involved in confrontations. I think that following Margaret (who was outgoing and attention seeking) in the birth order, Ruth found it easier (or safer) to be quietly in the background. I seem to remember her demeanor as being more like Maggie than any of the rest of us, as much as some of us wanted to be like mom. That I can see, no one truly succeeded.

On some things, my memory is foggy, but in my mind, I seem to recall Ruth as always being "starched." I think of crisp clothes... blouses and cotton dresses... when I think of Ruth. In my mind's eye, I see her as frequently being at the ironing board. Memory is a funny thing. There are sometimes specifics that come clearly while the big picture stays hidden behind a fog. I think none of us can be truly positive that any memory is actual, and not cultivated. However, we must go with what we have and try to be as precise as we can. That is what I am doing.

I don't have many clear memories of Ruth when I was very young. That might be because, like Margaret, she married and left home when I was very young… but unlike Margaret, Ruth did not have her first child until I was almost four years old. I am sure that at the age of four, I was far too busy to be bothered with a baby niece. I already had Joey, and doubt that either one of us could be bothered with Joyce. Joey and I were much too occupied and active to be involved with a baby! Even though Joyce was closer in age to Margaret's daughter, Joanne, I am pretty sure I was a much more exciting playmate.

Ruth eventually had five children, and I do remember her being a good and sensitive mom. The fact that she was the one, at one time, who saved me from what could have been serious burns, may have, consciously or subconsciously, endeared her to me… but that is a story for another chapter.

I would, at times, spend a weekend at Ruth's house when she lived in Pepperell, a neighboring town. For a young child, it was a fun place to be. There were no clear-cut rules, and she was easy-going, as was her husband, Martin, who could be very silly at times. He would make up far-fetched stories that I was never sure were truth or fabrication. Ruth would look at him, roll her eyes, and just say "Mah-tin, stop." There were not a lot of "don't do that" rules. I don't remember Ruth being bossy like some of my older sisters. She had a growing family of her own. During my visits, she may have been too busy doing the usual housework to pay much attention to what I was doing. She made sure that our activities were safe, but beyond that, she was a "go have fun, kids" type of mother. Most of all, I not only loved Ruth, I *liked* her.

Ruth became a victim of the insidious Alzheimer's disease, and died in April 1999 at the age of 83.

#3 ETHEL LOUISE... THE SEAMSTRESS

Ethel was born on June 14, 1917, when her elder sister, Ruth, was just 14 months old. With no disposable diapers and two babies still in diapers, plus a 3-year-old toddler, our mother was kept more than busy just keeping up with the laundry. She did not have a washing machine at that time but would use a scrubbing board, and she definitely did not have a dryer! Mother Nature dried the clothes outside on a line when the weather permitted. On stormy days, the clothes would be draped over a rack and dried inside. But I'm wandering. Back to Ethel.

Ethel was cute. She was talented. She was musical. She was also, for the most part, a pacifist. Though I did not know her when she was a child, I do have pictures of her when she was young. She had a little round face and a cowlick separating the front of her hair. That cowlick was and is an identifying mark of most of the Conner kids, and unfortunately, the mark of many of the generations that followed. No amount of wetting or hair glue can keep it tamed. But, even with her hated cowlick, Ethel was cute.

Ethel was sixteen when I was born. When I was a baby, she would take me, nearly every day, in the carriage for a walk up the street. This was not a chore, I am told, but something she chose to do and enjoyed doing.

She was a very gifted person who loved to play the piano, and in later years, the organ. She was adept at sewing, darning, knitting, and crocheting. She did make quite a few clothes for me when I was growing up. It was amazing to me that she could get an old dress, take it apart, and remake it into something that was cute and new to me.

When they were older, Ethel and Charlotte would, of course, hang out together. Ethel would often follow Charlotte's lead. That action frequently got her into trouble because Charlotte was (as you will later read) a hell-raiser and an instigator. She did, at least once get Ethel in trouble for literally "hanging out" with her.

One time, Ethel and Charlotte were in bed, supposedly sleeping, when they heard neighborhood kids, the Keefes, in the yard. (The Keefes were usually allowed to stay up later than our family was.) Charlotte and Ethel raised the high dormer window by standing on the bed, and with Charlotte holding up the window, they were both leaning out, talking to their friends. When Charlotte heard our father coming up the back stairs, she let go of the window (which came down), and quickly jumped down, got under the blankets and feigned sleep.

My father entered the room and saw the window closed down on Ethel. It was trapping her upper half outside the window and her bottom half inside, with her feet barely touching the bed. Mickey, before opening the window, gave her a swat on her butt, which was sticking out at a convenient swatting level. He then freed her from the stocks-like hold the window had on her, put her into bed, and left the room. Charlotte had pulled off another caper and gotten away with it, undetected, much to Ethel's dismay. This story became one of the many family classics. While Ethel did complain to Charlotte about the unfairness of being caught, she never "tattled." She was not a "get-even" type of person. She knew, even then, that though Charlotte was younger, Charlotte was the leader.

In her later years, after I was married, Ethel developed macular degeneration and eventually lost her vision. She was no longer able to work on the knitting and handcrafting that she so enjoyed, although she continued to try. The last pair of mittens she made for me had several holes where she had dropped stitches, but she presented them to me proudly. She could not see the holes and would have been embarrassed had she known. I accepted them with thanks and never told her.

Ethel passed away on July 29, 1998, at the age of 81.

#4 CHARLOTTE ALLISON... THE FEISTY ONE

Charlotte was born on December 31, 1919. Happy New Year to Maggie and Mickey! I think Charlotte was born feisty. She never, that I know of, backed down to anyone... tall or short, big or small, man or woman - and she's proud of it.

Charlotte was the fourth surviving child born to Maggie and Mickey. I think at that time my parents decided my father was never going to have a son to be his namesake, so they feminized his first name, Charles, and named her "Charlotte Allison Conner"... a name she professed to hate from (I think) the time she could first speak. She was an unabashed tomboy, but she also had a soft spot that not many people saw. When I was about six years old and in first grade, I tapped into that soft spot. The experience made Charlotte, for that period in time, my favorite sister.

Charlotte was around nineteen or twenty years old, and was, of course, working and dating. I was sharing the big double bed with her, and I would be in bed sleeping when she came home from a date. She would climb into bed and lightly shake me, snuggle me and then ask, "What did you do in school today, Ally?" I would tell her. Following my informational recitation, she would ask me if I had learned any new songs. She would then, in what seemed like the middle of the night to me, have me sing the songs that I had learned that day. If there were no new ones to offer, she would have me sing the ones I had learned on previous days or weeks.

This memory remains quite special to me even now. I can still, after 70+ years, remember the words to some of those songs and the special feeling I had when my "big sister" would snuggle me and listen to me sing, late into the night.

Charlotte is, as of this writing, 93 years old. She not only remembers my "singing nights," but I think she remembers every joke she ever heard. She gets great fun out of sometimes shocking the aged at her senior citizens group by entertaining them with an occasional slightly risqué joke. She hasn't changed a lot in all these years and will still verbally take on anyone necessary, if she feels she is right and they are wrong. The doctor, the "powers that be" in her town, or the postal delivery service have all been "corrected" by Charlotte. She is an amazing lady, one you are wise not to antagonize.

Charlotte tolerated little or no nonsense from the younger group in the family and this especially applied to brother Pat, who was high-spirited, to say the least, and always looking for a way to tease someone. Older sisters were easy prey because they usually had no patience with his antics.

A family story, many times validated by others, was that Charlotte was washing the kitchen floor and Pat, to get her riled, was frequently knocking, then opening the door from outside and placing a dirty foot onto her clean floor. She had warned him several times to stop, but to no avail. Her last warning was, "If you open that door one more time, you're going to get this mop in your face!" A few minutes of peace ensued, and then once again, a knock came on the kitchen door. Charlotte, without hesitation, quickly opened the door, and as promised, did in fact; put the mop in the face... of the insurance man who had come to collect his monthly premium. I am sure that Pat was around the corner of the porch, enjoying his sister's embarrassing dilemma. No doubt, Charl found a way to get even, eventually.

Such is the way with large families, and this story is the perfect example of how memories can differ. There was controversy between siblings I spoke to as to who the actual mop-holder was in the story, so I decided I needed to go directly to the source. I called Charlotte to ask her. She verified, laughingly, that she was indeed the one mopping the floor that day, and even gave me the name of the insurance man whose face had been the target of the sloppy mop. Even through disagreements, this story became one of the many family classics.

#5 STANLEY BENJAMIN… THE CLOWN "PAT"

Stanley Benjamin Conner, known to all as "Pat," was born on April 6, 1921. He was the fifth surviving child of Maggie and Mickey and (finally) the first male child.

Pat was mischievous and fun loving as a boy, and that trait never left him in his short life. It seemed the main goal in his growing-up years was to torment and tease his four older sisters. He loved to get them riled, and according to family stories, they seldom failed to respond in a way that would send him running away snickering before they could catch him.

Pat was, even as a teenager, tall and charming, with blonde wavy hair and smiling blue eyes. All… even the targeted older sisters he often plagued… loved him.

Pat was only twelve years old when I was born, and for the first several years of my life he barely acknowledged that I was alive. From the time I was six or seven, I adored this biggest brother.

Like all of the "Conner kids," Pat was musical. He played the harmonica and guitar, loved "cowboy" music, and would, at times, come ambling down Main Street, day or night, singing and yodeling at the top of his lungs. He also loved to dance, but he was most impressive when he was dancing on skates at the roller rink at Whalom Park, an amusement park in a nearby town.

I was probably seven or eight when Pat took me to the roller rink on a Saturday afternoon. Was it for a special occasion? I don't know. Pat was a very impulsive person, and he may have just decided that was the thing to do at the moment. This was a very big thrill in my young life! I had never been on roller skates, but he got me fitted and took me out on the floor, attempting to teach me how to skate. At the skating rink, the organ music was playing and people were all skating in time to the music, around the outside edge of the rink. To have an eight-year-old skittering and flopping was definitely interrupting the flow and rhythm of the crowd.

Pat reached down, picked me up, and said, "Hang on, Ally," and off he went, gliding around the floor with me, first in his arms and then on his shoulders. I felt like I was flying! I remember that I wasn't even frightened. I had complete faith in him. I knew I was not going to be dropped. He would not fall.

I think roller rinks are a thing of the past. I doubt that any of my children or grandchildren will ever have the experience of gliding around the floor on skates in time to the loud organ music. Probably, the closest they will come, will be at the local skate park doing high jumps and twists, while heavy metal music plays from a boom box in the background. I have to admit they amaze me and I love watching them (though I could do without the heavy metal music). Each generation has its own definition of joy and excitement.

Pat died in an automobile accident on February 6, 1951. He was 28 years old and left his wife, a six-year-old daughter, and an unborn son. His son was born two months after his death. We called him "Pat."

#6 LAWRENCE HARLOW … THE GREAT DEBATER "LARRY"

To most, he was "Larry," this middle child of Maggie and Mickey. Larry was born November 19, 1922. I always thought Larry was the typical middle child, and he had said that of himself.

Any family who has an odd number of children will have a middle child. We hear, most often, of the "middle" child of three children, but Larry was number six in eleven children. That made him about as middle as you can get, with five older and five younger. Though ten years older than I, Larry and I enjoyed many of the same things, and when I was older, Larry became my friend (and my future husband's friend)… so much so that he was best man at our wedding, and my first son was named after him… but that is another story.

I think nearly all, if not all, of the family called him "Larry." To me he was always "Laurie," and I am not sure how my pronunciation of his name came about. My children and grandchildren, however, have always referred to him as "Uncle Laurie" so "Laurie" is, for their benefit, how I shall refer to him in this writing.

Laurie was away in the Navy during a portion of WW II, and I would, sometimes, write letters to him. I am sure they were childish ramblings, but I think they must have meant much to a sailor stationed overseas or on a ship in the middle of a vast ocean. He didn't talk much about the war, but he did tell me that one time he saw a Kamikaze pilot coming toward the ship. He said the worst feeling he had ever had, was looking up and seeing a plane that was diving and deliberately aiming straight for his ship. I wanted to know if it had hit, veered off and missed, or was shot down but I didn't ask for details, and he volunteered nothing further.

Laurie came home from the war, alive but badly shell-shocked. I believe today that might be called "Post Traumatic Stress Disorder." It was as if his nerves were outside his skin with no insulation to help absorb light, sounds, or sudden movements. One time while we were sitting around the kitchen table chatting, he literally jumped up from his chair and paled, when someone slammed a door behind him. For a long time, he was hypersensitive to much of his surroundings.

When he was home, Laurie and I would sometimes sit at the old piano in the little back room, brother and sister playing duets and singing. Neither of us was great at the piano, but we both enjoyed playing together. Singing duets was the most fun, and Laurie had a nice mellow tenor voice that blended well with my contralto. At that time, we would play and sing old reminiscent songs like "Let The Rest of the World Go By" and duets such as "Harvest Moon." In later years, we had quite a repertoire of duets. "Baby It's Cold Outside" was one of our favorites… he would pick out the melody on the slightly out-of-tune old piano while I accompanied on the bass chords. He occasionally liked to throw in his own lyrics to make me laugh. Then we would carry on seeing who could outdo the other with the craziest words.

Laurie had a quiet, witty sense of humor, and would at times, make the most unexpected "comebacks." He loved, and was very good at playing horseshoes, cribbage, and doing crossword puzzles. Much to the dismay of most of the men and boys in the family, he would most often be the winner at horseshoes. To beat Laurie was quite a coup.

Laurie loved to argue and would go to great lengths to get a good debate started. In some ways, he was the Archie Bunker of the family: sensitive most of the time, annoying a lot of the time, and loved all of the time.

Laurie died in April 1995 at the age of seventy-three.

#7 HELEN MAY... THE GARBAGE COLLECTOR

Helen was born October 31, 1924. Happy Halloween Maggie and Mickey! Was she a trick or a treat?

Sister Helen became the official garbage collector in the family, and she did that job for quite a long time, though I could not put a number of weeks, months or years on how long she did it. I say she "became" the official collector because brother Larry was the first appointed to that job. Her job, at that time, was doing dishes. Helen told me that she hated doing dishes and that Larry, in turn, did not like collecting garbage. So they made a deal. He would do the dishes if she would collect the garbage. For some reason (I think it must have been temporary insanity) she agreed and became the official garbage collector.

Now, when I say "garbage collector," I mean exactly that! We had pigs that needed to be fed and while they did, I am sure, get portions of corn or grain each day, I think Mickey might have felt that they needed extra scraps to fill them up. Things such as potato peels, carrot tops, and other cooking scraps were saved and dumped into the pigs' trough. I doubt though, there was much food to scrape off the plates after a meal was finished at our house. There were, however, in our small village, families that did have leftovers, and thus each day, Helen would take a metal garbage pail by the handle, walk up the street, and stop at neighbors' houses. They would empty the food scraps they had saved into her pail, and then she would carry the full pail home, and dump it in for the pigs. They would, of course, grunt, snort, squeal, and push at each other as they gobbled it up. In a large family, there is not usually much food left over after meals, but our pigs, thanks to the neighbors and Helen, fared well.

In the summer it was not a problem because there were many scraps left from the garden, such as corncobs, skins, peels and other unpalatable things that were separated from the vegetables as they were being prepared. Our pigs were big, lean and tasty.

I look at sister Helen today... successful, always nicely dressed and beautifully coiffed... and I have to suppress a giggle when I picture her carrying a garbage pail up Main Street in Townsend Harbor.

#8 JEAN ELIZABETH...
THE CLOTHES HORSE

Jean was born on August 9, 1926. Jean, seven years older than I, was a puzzle to me much of the time that I was growing up. I was never sure if she liked me or not. In retrospect, I think <u>she</u> was not sure, either, a lot of the time. Looking back, as an adult, I can understand that she may well have been ambivalent regarding this newest member of the family.

Jean was cute, with light brown hair and a round, freckled face. She had been the "baby girl" for seven years. I imagine she was babied and indulged by the older sisters, since her birth had been followed by two rowdy boys. Then I came along and usurped her spot as "the baby girl," moving her to simply "the eighth child in a large family." I, too, would have had mixed emotions. She would stand up for me when someone was picking on me, but minutes later, she might be the one picking on me because "Ally never has to do the dishes" or some other such thing. She tried to explain to me about how my first menstrual period would be, but I refused to listen. I just knew she was making up that bizarre story! We did, however, become good friends, sharing a love for music, cooking, and many other things.

#8 JEAN ELIZABETH...THE CLOTHES HORSE

When I think of Jean, I think of clothes and shoes, for I know of no one who loved clothes and shoes more. (Well, maybe Imelda Marcos, but she could better afford them.) Jean attempted to be a fashion plate at a young age, from what I am told. She enjoyed the minis, the maxis, the ball length, sparkles, spangles... whatever the style of the day was, she would try to wear it.

This desire to be fashionable was not always possible, as you can see in the picture of the five youngest children posing with our mother. That outfit may have been one of Jean's earliest creations. In my imagination, I can hear them now, announcing it on the fashion runway: "*...our next model is wearing a topless sun suit with long, irregular spaghetti straps. The short, unevenly rolled cuffed pants, complete the outfit.*" It was an original creation, for sure. Jean was only about ten years old when that picture was taken and was already showing a flair for original design.

I was told that when Jean was growing up she would, of necessity, at times "redesign" her outfit on her way to school. One story goes that she had received a beautiful new red, hooded jacket... probably for Christmas. This was a warm, long jacket reaching down to about fingertip length. Her skirt would have hung a bit below the jacket.

Our mother liked seeing us dressed as well as possible, but warmth was the ultimate goal for her children when they were walking to the corner and waiting for the school bus in weather that was frequently, in winter, below zero. Jean was instructed to wear heavy woolen socks, knee high, for added warmth. This was not stylish! Not with a beautiful new red jacket! On the way to the corner, in silent protest, Jean rolled her socks down to her ankles (and may have hitched her skirt up) to let her bare legs show, sacrificing warmth for style. I doubt it was stylish at that time to have dark-colored wool socks in a roll around your ankles, but in her mind, she was gorgeous, with her bare legs likely turning a motley shade of reddish-blue by the time the bus arrived.

Like most of us, Jean played the piano by ear. I remember her coming home and showing me, on the piano, a "new song" she had heard…"'Til The End of Time." I learned to play the song, and it was a few years later that I discovered that it was originally Chopin's "Polonaise." I wanted to surprise her with this new knowledge, so I spent much time, unsuccessfully, trying to master it as Chopin had written it.

As adults, especially after both of us had been widowed, Jean and I became closer. I discovered that she could be zany, but sometimes needed an instigator to get her going. I was only too happy to play that role… I had been practicing that most of my life.

As with all of the "Conner kids", music became one of our strongest bonds.

#9 HENRY JAMES... MR CLEAN "JIM"

I believe "Jim" has been making significant marks on the family since the day he was born on October 25, 1929. The child before him, Jean, was three years old when Jim was born. The time between Jean and Jim was the longest our mother had gone without being pregnant, for between all the others there were two years, or less.

I can't say that Jim was bad to me as we were growing up... at least no worse than any other brother who had a sister four years younger. I do believe, though, that he was the originator of the many names I was called... none of them very complimentary. "Ding-Toed-Ally," "Bucktooth Ally," or "Knock-kneed-Ally" were a few of his choice taunts. I think it is because of him, however, that I now walk correctly instead of tripping over my own feet, as I often did when I was young because my feet toed in so badly. I couldn't do anything about the buckteeth or the knock-knees, but I do remember concentrating on walking with my toes pointed out, kind of like a duck, so that he would not call me "Ding-Toed-Ally" anymore. It worked. Thanks, Jim!

As a youngster, he was inventive. A doll carriage that I had was sacrificed, unbeknownst to me at the time, to fuel his inventiveness. Jim was probably the one who decided that a wagon would be much more useful than a doll carriage, so he proceeded to dismantle my doll carriage and turn some of the parts into a wagon. Chuck professes to being part of that scene, but since Chuck has never been very mechanical, I strongly suspect that Jim was the mastermind of the "doll carriage caper."

Inactivity is a word that, I believe, has never been in Jim's vocabulary. If he sits down for very long, when he finally stands up, you can be sure he will have completed the carving of a knick-knack such as a Santa Claus for your collection, or made a lawn ornament, or perhaps created a plaque for your wall. Skilled, talented, energetic, and dependable, is this ninth child in the Conner clan.

Jim has always had a lot of energy and, even as a boy, found jobs to do. He would take jobs that no one else wanted, and with little complaint, do them, no matter how difficult or dirty. Cleaning chicken houses was one such job that sticks in my mind. I don't know how old he was when a local man who raised chickens hired him. Jim's job was to go over to the chicken farm early each morning, before school, and clean out the henhouses. Most of you are probably unaware of the amount of droppings even a <u>dozen</u> hens can produce overnight, and even more unaware of just how odoriferous their droppings can be. This man had many more than a dozen chickens. Jim would spend the early hours shoveling out chicken manure from the henhouses, and then come home, clean up, eat breakfast, and head to the corner to catch the school bus.

"Cleaning up" in those days was a bit more than coming in and hopping in the shower, since we had no shower or even a bathroom. Cleaning up meant taking a basin of water to your room, with facecloth, towel, and soap, and washing yourself thoroughly. Your other option was to fill the basin and wash up in the kitchen at the sink. Whichever Jim's choice was, I was unaware for a long time that Jim was aiming for "Clorox clean" in his morning ablutions. I was unaware, that is, until one morning we climbed on the school bus and I heard a girl from one of the "better" families in town say to another girl, "It's at this stop that we first smell it. I knew that smell came from one of them." And from my seat behind her, I saw her elbow her friend and point to Jim as he walked by their seat.

"It's him," she whispered. Of course I had no idea what she was talking about but then, on the alert, I sniffed and sure enough...Clorox fumes were emanating from Jim. I am sure he was cleaning his hands thoroughly with Clorox after getting home from cleaning the henhouses and before leaving for school. Any of us who have used Clorox know how difficult it is to remove the smell. Not so bad, though, if you think of what the alternate odor might have been.

I can't remember if I told him what the girls had said or not. I might have waited until one day when he was name-calling, and then thrown him the zinger..."Yeah, well all the kids say you smell like bleach!" I really hope I dealt with it that way. Wish I could remember.

#10 CHARLES ALLISON JR. … THE (milk) PITCHER ("CHUCK")

This last boy and tenth child to be born to my parents was named after my father, but during most of his early years was called "Junior"… a name that was most often shortened to "Junie." As soon as he was old enough to make the decision on his own, "Junior" was changed to "Charles" or "Charlie." I suspect that was when he started school. Even then though, the immediate neighborhood population still referred to him as "Junie." He had a hard time shucking that name.

He was probably in or around the sixth grade when he started to be called "Charlie" by his peers, but "Junie" prevailed at home for a long time. I seem to remember that it was after he moved away from home that he decided to be called "Chuck." I could never figure out why my parents waited until this tenth child to have declared a namesake for Mickey. "Charlotte Allison" came pretty close, but perhaps they felt they wanted the masculine accuracy. Maybe they thought this would be their last child and so chose him to carry on my father's name. Just another question I wish I had asked.

Chuck, being only 19 months older than I, has a lot of space in my memory pool.. He hated to lose (and still does)... especially to a younger sister who even had the nerve to learn to ride a bike before he did! A very vivid memory, one familiar to almost all of the family, is the first to surface. Chuck always loved sports and played on the baseball and basketball teams in our little high school. He loved to pitch and had a pretty good arm. That was demonstrated at an early age at our supper table one evening when he was approximately seven years old. I would have been around five. Some sort of an altercation prior to being called to the table probably provoked the incident I am about to describe. In retrospect, I also suspect that, whatever the disagreement had been, I had turned out the winner, and he was still angry.

Our supper table was square and quite large, taking up a good portion of the center of the kitchen. We all had our own places at which we sat at each meal. I sat to the left of my mom, and just around the corner of the table, to my left, sat Chuck.

On this particular day, we were all at our places, food on our plates, milk glasses filled. I was busy eating when I heard a whisper from my left.

"Baby," he whispered. I ignored it.

"Baby, baby," he persisted, just loud enough so only I could hear. Once again, I ignored it.

"Baby, baby, baby."

That was it! "Mom," I whined, "Junie's calling me 'baby'."

"Junior, stop now and eat your supper," she said quietly and firmly. A few moments went by with the usual supper table patter going on. Then, while staring innocently at his plate, he started again, "Baby, baby."

Okay! Too much! I quickly moved my left elbow at the next "baby" whisper. It came in contact with his milk glass, which didn't tip over, but "sloshed" out over the top and onto his plate. In a split second, he grabbed the glass and threw the rest of the milk directly into my face. Dead on hit!

"M-a-a-m-a!" I yelled at the top of my lungs as milk dripped off my eyelashes, down my face and onto my shirt. My mother pushed back her chair and stood, pointing to each of us in turn, "You," to Chuck, "upstairs," her pointer finger swung toward the shed door. "You," to me, finger pointing to the front, "upstairs."

Chuck headed to the door leading to the back stairs and I, of course, to the door leading to the front, while the rest of the family sat quietly with their mouths agape, unbelieving that Junie would have dared do such a thing… especially at the supper table.

While I was on my bed, maybe an hour later, my mother came up with a plate of food for me. I never knew if she brought a plate to him or not, but I strongly suspect that she did. If he didn't get food, he certainly got bragging rights for some time after the incident. All who knew him heard that he had "got me good!"

In later years, Chuck and I became closer, and in fact, were cast as "lovers" in one of our high school musicals. Even though we were friends, that was hard. Can you imagine having to hold hands with your brother and look lovingly into his eyes while you sang a romantic duet? Sing it we did, and successfully, but underneath, both of our reactions were…ugh!

#11 ALLY ARRIVES

I was born on May 7, 1933, in a hospital in Fitchburg, Massachusetts. It was a Sunday, and I know that is a fact because I looked it up on a century calendar. I was told at some point in my life that I was born on Mother's Day, but I know that is not possible since Mother's Day always falls on the second Sunday in May, and it just doesn't work with the calendar. I do know, however, that it was the Sunday before Mother's Day, which I thought was okay until I became a mother. I then found out it is rather like being born the week before Christmas. My Mother's Day greetings and gifts are always kind of lumped in with my birthday, so I feel like I get gypped out of one or the other.

I really didn't mind being born on a Sunday, though, because my mother frequently used to recite to me the lines of an age-old poem that said:

Monday's child is fair of face
Tuesday's child is full of grace
Wednesday's child is full of woe
Thursday's child has far to go
Friday's child is loving and giving
Saturday's child works hard for a living…

And then came the clincher that I loved:
But the child that is born on the Sabbath day,
Is bonnie and blithe and bright and gay!

When I was very small and first heard that poem, I had no idea what all the words meant, but I knew from the way she said it that it was something good. I also have to add that in those days "*gay*" simply meant "*happy*" and had no sexual connotations.

I probably could have entitled this section "Lil' Nana Arrives" but Lil' Nana didn't really come into existence until sometime in the early 1980s when my first grandchild, Eric, needed a name to differentiate me from (at that time) his many other grandmothers. When he was born, he had two great-grandmothers, and two grandmothers. He was having difficulty making people understand which grandmother he was referring to. One day when speaking of "Nana," he said, "I know. I can call you Lil' Nana." His parents liked that and so Lil' Nana I became. The laughs came when his maternal grandmother, Sally Jones, got the word. Her comment? "You can call her Lil' Nana…that's fine with me. Just don't think you're going to be calling me 'Big Nana'!" (She quickly became Nana Jones, which has since been shortened to Nana J.)

I have remained Lil' Nana, not only to my grandchildren and great-grandchildren, but also to the offspring of their friends.

Never underestimate the power of children!

PART II
OUR HOUSE IN THE HARBOR

THE BIG BLACK STOVE

When I think of our house in "The Harbor," there are some things that stand out in my mind, and the big, black "pot-belly stove" in the living room is one of those things.

That stove was our main source of heat. Because of that, on some very cold winter mornings, the living room became a dressing room for some of us. I would wake up snuggled under warm blankets in the upstairs bedroom. The temperature outside could be as cold as 30 degrees below zero. Sometimes there was ice on the inside of the windows. I would get out of bed, make a beeline down the front stairs to the living room, and stand as close to the big old stove as I could get to absorb that wonderful heat before going into the kitchen for breakfast.

In the kitchen was the cooking stove that was heated by two oil burners. These burners were fed oil from a giant bottle that hung upside down on some kind of a stand in the far back corner of the stove. From that bottle, a line, sort of a tube-like thing, ran to the burners. Every once in a while you would hear a "glug, glug, glug," and if you looked at the bottle when you heard that noise, you would see bubbles rising up in the bottle. When the bottle got nearly empty, someone (not me) would take the bottle out to the shed and refill it from an oil barrel.

But, back to the living room stove. This stove was very important at Christmas time. I, and maybe the others when they were young, would make a wish list for Santa Claus, and then on Christmas Eve my mother would look at the list, and then open the stove door and throw the list into the fire. I really believed that the note would go up the chimney, and Santa would get it when he landed on the roof. He would then check my list and bring me whatever he had in his sleigh to give me. Pretty weird what kids believe, but I was always, even as a child, one who had a vivid imagination… magical thinking came easily to me.

I was quite young, pre-school age, when the old stove let me know that it was not to be messed with! I remember my sister Ruth was having tea at the kitchen table with my mother, when I decided to put something in the stove. I opened the door, and somehow my shirt caught on fire. Of course, I let out a yell and Mom and Ruth came running in. Ruth grabbed me, and quickly wrapped her arms around me in a bear hug and smothered the fire. Ruth must have acted almost instinctively. I don't remember being treated for burns or anything afterwards, but I do know that I never opened that stove door again until I was considerably older.

UPSTAIRS...THREE BEDROOMS, MANY KIDS

One of my first memories is of being in a crib in my parents' bedroom. I have no idea how many years I slept in that crib, but I remember a cat's climbing into the crib with me and my mother's shooing it out. The bedroom was located over the kitchen and was a reasonable size, but not what I would consider a large room. As I remember it, there was a double bed in the room and a bureau with a large mirror. (There may have been two bureaus or dressers, but I don't remember a second one.) My parents' bed took up half the room, and against the wall opposite their bed was my crib. The crib was snugged in under a sloping ceiling. To this day, I love bedrooms with sloping ceilings. The crib occupied the space that would, in my later years, hold the "big box," which I will explain later.

There were two doors into my parents' room. One door went into a back hall and to the back stairs that led down to the shed, which in turn led to the kitchen. That upstairs back hall also led to the "boys bedroom." The other door led into the front, the "girls bedroom," and then into a front hall and down stairs to the living room.

I never figured out just why my parents chose to take the middle bedroom. Perhaps it was because it not only separated the boys from the girls, but also gave Mom easy access to all children in times of childhood illnesses and feverish nights. It could also have been because the front bedroom, being the largest, was needed by the girls since there was a passel of them. Then again, it might have been because the middle room was the warmest room upstairs, having been built with a grate in the floor that was located just over the kitchen stove. The heat would rise up through that grate to give some semblance of warmth the other upstairs rooms lacked. I never asked. I guess I'll never know.

THE GIRLS' ROOM

I don't remember at what age I was moved out of my parents' room and into the "girls' room." This room was the big bedroom in the upstairs front of the house. It was, indeed, a large room. It had two large windows in the front overlooking the front lawn, the street, and the leatherboard mill where my father worked. There were two large windows on one side wall that overlooked the porch and the field between our house and the house next door. On a third wall was the door to my parents' room and next to that door, a fireplace and then a closet. The fireplace was never used as a heat source, so it was a great place to hide things (such as love letters etc.) because there was a little shelf-like area just up inside the chimney. The fourth wall was unbroken, with the exception of the door at one end that led to the upstairs hall. That door provided access to the front stairs that led to a fairly large downstairs hall and then into the living room.

I remember that at one time, this room held two double beds and a cot, but in most of my growing-up years, it held a double bed and a single bed. It was a nice, bright room, but like the rest of the upstairs rooms, it had no heat. The only heat we had was what might escape from the living room underneath, if the downstairs hall door was left open. In short, in winter it was a very cold room, although I will say it was never as cold as the boys' room, which was built over the shed.

At one time there was a double bed that one or two of my sisters slept in and next to that was the cutest thing you ever saw. It was a miniature double bed that was made of brass. You are probably wondering why anyone would want a miniature double bed. Well, my father worked for some interesting people when he did part-time carpentry work, and I think the most interesting of all were "the midgets." You may refer to them as "little people" now to be politically correct, but in those days, they were simply referred to by all, including themselves, as "the midgets."

These little people were a married couple who stood about 3' or 31/2' tall like Tom Thumb, and performed with the circus. They had a summer/weekend home across the bridge in Townsend Harbor and they used to have my father do carpentry work for them. I believe a wealthy elderly lady for whom my father later did much work, owned this house. I don't have a lot of memories of the midgets except that their house was the neatest place a kid could possibly visit. All the furniture was small, to fit their size, and it was rather like walking into a house that was made just for me, because I was just about their size.

How or why did my father end up with this little brass bed? It may have been given to him in payment for a job he did, or perhaps it was just going to be discarded and so he salvaged it. I only know he brought it home for me, and I slept in it until I outgrew it… which wasn't more than a year or two. I don't know whatever happened to that little bed. I'll have to add it to my "I'll never know" list, but if anyone has it now, it is probably worth a great deal of money. It will never be worth more than the memory of it… and the knowledge that my father brought it home for me.

PEE-UP-ME-BACK-ALLY

There are a few memories that everyone in the family seems to agree on with minimal variations. I was called "Ally," not "Alice," from the time I can remember, by most of the family. The story goes that when I was very small, if I should cry at night, my mother would bring me into bed, and I would snuggle up against my father's back and go back to sleep. Of course, those were the days of rubber sheets, but before plastic pants or disposable diapers, and so if I wet while sleeping, it would soak into my father's nightclothes. When he would get up in the morning after one of those watery nights, he would greet me with, "Here's old Pee-Up-Me-Back-Ally". That is still one of the many stories that is repeated and laughed at in our family, even after 70+ years have gone by. The amazing thing is, everyone agrees on that story.

Mickey was a small man. At least he was small of stature. I never knew anyone who thought he was small in any other way. As far as I knew, he was a very honest man and took no nonsense from anyone who wasn't. He ruled his family with a very firm hand and a loud voice that could make you feel as though you were in the presence of a man twice his size. He stood about 5'4" or maybe a little more, but what he lacked in size, he made up for in gusto, spunk, and spirit.

Mickey was everybody's best friend. Everyone who met him was an instant friend, and I knew no one who had a bad word to say about him. Now that I think about it, they wouldn't have said it to me anyway. He had many friends and acquaintances, and the only people I ever heard bad-mouth him were in his own family. If I think back and am really honest with myself (and you), I was afraid of him, but mixed in with that fear were two feelings that I did not realize until I was much older: respect and awe.

Mickey was a very strict father. If you think of the times and the circumstances, along with the number of kids and responsibilities, he would not have been able to survive if he had not been as tough as he was...both physically and mentally. I believe that hidden beneath that tough façade was a man very proud of his kids, but who never learned to say that. He was also, under the façade, a very sensitive man. He was able to hide his sensitive side most of the time, but on occasion, it would come through. I know it came through for me.

Strangely enough, I was still in the womb when he first showed his sensitive side toward me. I am repeating this story as it was told to me. There was a man who had a little shop a couple of miles down the road from us. His name was Frank, and in his shop he sold wicker furniture. I have a vague memory of his shop, on the corner of Airport Road, (that is what we used to call it since there was a small airstrip there). I don't know if it is actually named Airport Road or not, since I haven't checked it out in many years. My memory of Frank himself is even more vague.

Before I was born, my father had Frank make (or order) a wicker bassinette for me to sleep in when my mom brought me home from the hospital. My father may have traded some carpentry work for this bassinette. He may have paid cash for it. Just another thing I will never know, but, either way, I know he probably needed the money more than he needed a wicker bassinette that I would outgrow in three or four months tops! Also, if I think about it, there were other things Frank had for sale that were wicker... probably more sensible items. I just think that Mickey's well-hidden sensitivity bubbled up, and before he could control it, it spilled out in an order to have a baby bassinette made.

I'm glad it did spill out. I love that bassinette, and some of my grandchildren have slept in it. My granddaughter, Kasey, now has that bassinette. I hope some of my great-grandchildren will sleep in it. It means a lot to me. I treasure things that are old. Someone may make a reproduction of that bassinette, but a new one will never be the same; it will never be the one Lil' Nana slept in.

DOUBLE BED, DOUBLE TROUBLE

When I was about five or six years old, I used to sleep in the big double bed with my sister Charlotte, who was about 14 years older than I. I think that at one time or another in my life, if questioned, I would have named each of my sisters as a "favorite," depending on my age and theirs at the time...Charlotte was my favorite then.

She was of working/dating age, which meant that she had a few extra dollars in her pocket. Because of that, she would occasionally treat me to a new blouse or a little bauble. Plus, she was very good at hugging, and I loved to be hugged. (I still do.)

When I was around eight or ten, I slept in that same bed with Helen, who was about eight years older than I. In the other bed slept sister Jean. Helen and I would get into bed and start giggling about some silly thing, and Jean, trying to go to sleep, would get very annoyed with us. When Jean started to complain that we were keeping her awake, it would cause us to giggle even more, making Jean angrier, until finally, she would threaten to tell our father.

This threat would usually keep us quiet for a few minutes and we would, huddled together under the covers (a nine-year-old and a seventeen-year-old), shake with silent laughter. We would hold our breaths and try not to allow the laughter to escape, until finally one of us could stand it no longer and would let go with a sound that resembled a combination of a loud exhalation and a whinny. When one of us let go with this noise (that was followed immediately with a loud, gasping for breath, inhaling sound), the other would burst into spasms of laughter, and so the whole thing would begin again. This time, however, Jean would yell down the stairs, "Pa, they won't stop fooling so I can sleep," which would be followed by my father's voice yelling in reply, just two words, "CAN IT!" That was always enough of a threat to stop us from any further horseplay. When Mickey yelled, "CAN IT!" nobody ever questioned or protested. That was the end, period! (At least until some future night when the whole scenario might very well be replayed.)

THE GRATE IN THE BEDROOM FLOOR

Ah yes, the grate in the bedroom floor. For you youngsters, who have grown up in times of central heating, let me explain the grate.

In long-ago times, there was no heat in the upstairs rooms of many houses. Putting a grate in the floor was a way of transporting heat to upstairs rooms. I suspect that at times it was a bane to my poor mother's existence… especially since it was situated just over the kitchen stove. The stove, you see, was a large, black cast-iron beast that was, in earlier days, fed with wood or coal. In my earliest memory, it was connected to the "oil bottle." There were no gas jets or electric rings as we see on stoves today, but just a large, flat top with round, flat iron plates that set into the top. You would set your pans on the top, and the heat from the wood, oil or coal burning inside the stove would cook your food, as well as heat the kitchen. The grate, which was in the ceiling directly above the stove, was flush with the ceiling. It was metal and had a design of a star in it that had holes to allow the heat to rise into the upstairs.

Our house was old and had settled, as houses do. This settling caused the floors to slant slightly downhill toward the grate, and while the holes in the grate allowed things (such as heat, steam, etc.) to go up, it also allowed things to come down into the kitchen through the holes. Usually, things that came down through the holes were liquids and occasionally, albeit very seldom, urine was the liquid.

As everyone knows, if you spill liquid, it will run to the lowest point. In this case, the lowest point in the bedroom belonging to my parents was at the end of the room, where the grate was located, just in front of the bureau.

Now, on the side of the bed (and tucked just a little bit under), the chamber pot (also known as a "pee pot" or "thunder jug") was located. The reason for this very important piece of equipment was that, first of all, the temperature in Townsend Harbor was known to drop to forty degrees below zero in the wintertime. Our house had no central heating and was at best, poorly insulated, (if insulated at all). If avoidable, you did not want to have to make a trip in the middle of the night to empty your bladder, because conditions could make it a very long and cold trip down the back stairs through the shed to the old "two-holer". It could also be a very dark walk, since in those days there was not a light switch on every wall to illuminate an area before you entered. *There was no light at all in the toilet!*

At any rate, there peeking out from under the bed was the pot. This pot was emptied and cleaned every morning, but that usually happened after everyone was off to school or work. When the house was emptied of people, my mother would go upstairs to perform her daily task of making beds and straightening up, which included emptying and cleaning the pot. On an occasional morning, however, one or more of us might be in her room, looking for an article of clothing in the big box, or perhaps just generally fooling around. It could, at one of these times, be that somebody's foot might accidentally kick the pot and, even if it didn't tip over, it might slosh enough so that a trickle of urine would run across the floor and head downhill toward the grate. It has been my experience that when a liquid spills, you can never move quickly enough to stop it from ending up in a place where it isn't wanted. In this case, that place was the grate.

An unwritten law of big families is, "If you know someone is going to be blamed, and you don't want it to be you, you must accuse the other guy quickly, loudly and clearly." Exercising that rule, anyone who was in the room at that time would immediately yell, "*You kicked the pot!*" and somehow, as urine trickled down through the star-shaped holes and onto the stovetop, you had absolved yourself.

Meanwhile, down in the kitchen, my mom would have been alerted to the impending disaster, either by the accusatory shout from above, or maybe, by this time, by the " s-s-s-t" noise that was followed by a small cloud of urine-smelling steam that was arising from the stove.

It seems to me that my mother seldom got upset over this infrequent happening, but simply reached for the dried coffee and proceeded to wipe the excess liquid off the top of the stove. She would then sprinkle a liberal amount of the coffee on the affected spot and the house would quickly begin to smell like a Chase & Sanborn factory instead of a men's urinal. This action might be followed by a call for us to stop fighting and get ready for school, or a demand that we go out in the yard if we were going to fight. It may have happened, but I don't remember any punishment being doled out for the "pot sloshing."

The grate in the floor of the bedroom served another important function. Strange as it may seem, it saved on my mother's voice in the morning, as well as allowing heat to seep up from the kitchen. My mother always rose early to make my father's breakfast. He had to be at work at 7 a.m., but fortunately for him, he worked just across the street in the leatherboard factory and could be at work in less than one minute from the time he left the back door. Mom would have the coffee made, his egg prepared, and would then take the broom handle and precisely at 6:45, she would tap the end of the broom handle on the star-shaped metal grate above the stove. My father would answer the tapping with a sleepy, "I'm up," and then jump out of bed and into his work clothes, and come down the back stairs into the kitchen. Just inside the kitchen door, he would stop at the sink, splash some water on his face and proceed to the table where Mom would have his eggs and coffee waiting for him.

When I think of the perfect timing of this daily morning scenario, it seems pretty impressive. Papa didn't like anything that was very hot, but from the time he got out of bed and down the stairs, washed, and to the table, the temperature of his eggs and coffee was usually perfect for him to eat quickly. He would then rise from the table, don his jacket (if in winter) and walk across the street to work. All of this was accomplished with perfect synchronization in a fifteen-minute period. It was as though an expert had choreographed it. The scene was exactly the same, five days a week, for all the years while I was growing up in that house.

JOEY AND I

I was less than two years old when I became an aunt. My oldest sister, Margaret (19 years older than I), had the first of the many nieces and nephews that were to follow. As I had six older sisters and four older brothers, it was a given that there would be many more. Margaret named this first niece "Joanne," and "Joey" and I were to become playmates, fast friends, and competitors for the many years that followed. Joey and I were, at times, closer than sisters. We were closer in age than I was to any of my sisters. We never thought of each other as aunt and niece, and spent much of our first years together playing and getting in trouble.

Joanne had, from my first memory of her, beautiful curly hair and from the beginning, as much as I loved her, I hated those ringlets! I also resented the fact that she "stole" my eldest sister from me.

Until Joey was born, Margaret was like my second mother. Suddenly, not only had I been replaced with another child, but one with beautiful curls! There was no way I could compete, and nothing I could do or say to divert attention to me when people would see us together. Their first remark would be, "Look at those beautiful curls," as they looked past me and focused on Joanne.

Although I was too small to realize what "don't get mad, get even" meant, that is precisely what I chose to do one day when we were playing upstairs in my mother's bedroom. I believe we were supposed to be up there taking a nap. Naptime was seldom used for sleeping. We found early on that if we were quiet enough, we could get in a great deal of playing during that two-hour period. No one bothered to check on us when we were (supposedly) sleeping, and so we learned to be quietly innovative in our play.

I was probably around four or five and Joey, of course, about three, so I was much more inventive, and she was young enough to be easily led. I think I must have come to the realization that I was never going to have beautiful curls, and no matter how hard I prayed, Joanne's curls were never going to fall out or become straight. It was up to me to take matters into my own hands.

"Let's play beauty parlor," I told her, and of course she agreed. "You be the customer first," I directed, as I went to my mother's bureau for the comb and scissors. I am sure you can picture the rest of the scene, but I'll tell you anyway. While Joey sat there on the edge of my parents' bed, I proceeded to cut off all those hated curls and left her hair unevenly chopped and about an inch or two long all over her head. When I was finished, she no longer had those long ringlets, but looked more like a newly shorn poodle with tiny, tight curls close to her head.

Joey stood up and said, "Okay, now it's your turn," to which I quickly replied, "I don't want to play this anymore. Let's play something else." She usually went along with my ideas and, thankfully, this time was no exception. We went on to play something else, but later, when my sister saw Joey's haircut, I was banned from playing with Joey for several days. If Margaret could have her way, and had my mother not intervened, my head probably would have been shaved!

THE BIG BOX

As I said earlier, the "big box" sat in the corner of my parents' bedroom. It was in the spot that my crib had occupied in earlier years. The "big box" wasn't anything special, but my oldest sister, Margaret, told me that my father had made the big box for storage. It was a wooden box, quite nicely finished, that measured about 28" x 34" and was about 25" high. When I wrote this story, the big box was still in my possession and I actually measured it for size.

When I was small, along with various articles of seasonal and/or outgrown clothing (waiting for someone else to grow into), were the minstrel costumes and wigs. (I will explain the minstrels a bit later in another chapter). What a great time we would have when we sneaked up and put on those costumes! Especially the wigs!

My niece, Joey, and I had quite a few good times with those costumes. It was a child's paradise, but we had to be alert because we were not supposed to play with them. We, of course, did our best not to get caught. At times, we would get into the big box when we were sent upstairs to take a nap, and at other times, we would sneak upstairs when my mom was busy. We would put on wigs and a satin (or some kind of shiny) shirt with sparkles on it and pretend, in front of the mirror, that we were famous actresses on stage.

We both were quite "hammy" when it came to acting, singing, and/or dancing, so the costumes made it complete for us. The only drawback was that, usually, we were supposed to be taking a nap, and we had to do it all in a very quiet way so as to not let my mother know we were awake and getting into the big box.

Besides costumes and hand-me-downs, the big box held other interesting articles. At one time, someone gave my mother a red fox collar (or maybe it was called a "stole"). I don't know if the collar originally came with a coat, but by the time it ended up in the big box, it was just the collar. It was pretty neat to me. It was a long, skinny piece of fur and actually had a fox head on one end and a tail on the other. I seem to think it also had some little tiny feet on it too.

It was, I think, mostly to be decorative and not a collar for warmth, but you would wrap it around your neck, and the mouth had a clip to open it. You would clip the mouth to the tail, and it stayed on your neck. I used to love to put that on and parade around. Today, if one wore that, she might be doused with paint or something because the extremists are so into saving every living creature, they sometimes violently protest the wearing of animal skins.

The big box could have told many stories if it could talk.

I rescued the big box from being thrown out, and saved it in my attic in the house in Montgomery, New York, and then later moved it with me to Vermont. Sadly, I had to part with it when I left Vermont. It was a rather large, cumbersome thing and needed an attic or a space where it could nestle under the eaves in an old house. It was given to a large family in Vermont to be used for storage, and I like to think that potential hand-me-downs are still being kept in it.

ONE SIZE LARGER, PLEASE

Some of my brothers and sisters will tell you that we were poor and that they always knew it. I know now, and have known for many years that we were poor, but somehow, as a child growing up and even as a teenager, I truly never thought of us as being poor. I also realize that being the last child, things were not as bad when I was growing up as they were for some of the older group. I know that there were always hand-me-down clothes and that shoes were only bought at certain times of the year. We got new shoes at Easter, again in September before school started, and usually some time during the winter. Summer was, for the most part, barefoot days.

Getting a new pair of shoes was such a treat that I never thought about NOT getting them... only about what a great thing it was to get them. I was reminded of this just a few weeks ago when I heard a young mother telling her child, around age nine, that they were going shopping for new shoes that afternoon. The child was complaining that she didn't want to go. " Couldn't we go some other day?" she begged. I couldn't help but think back on how exciting it was for us to get new shoes, and even more exciting to get to go to the store and pick our own.

I know it probably sounds strange, but my parents often went shopping for our shoes without us. They would take one of our shoes with them. (Sometimes they took one shoe of each of three or four kids to the store in Fitchburg.) There was no Payless Shoe Store type of place, or large stores with shoe departments that I know of. Just independently owned shoe shops. Anyway, my parents would take one of our shoes in and get the next size up. They usually did this when they went shopping on a Saturday night. When we woke up on Sunday morning, we would have new shoes. It was pretty exciting!

SIDE BY SIDE

When most people think of a "toilet" or "outhouse" or "two-holer" they think of a small room that is smelly and unpleasant, a place that you would not go into unless you had absolutely no choice. If a choice were given, you would probably choose to go out in the woods to deposit your bodily wastes… especially if you had been a person who had been lucky enough to experience a bathroom prior to being exposed to a "toilet." Our toilet was no exception. It was small and smelly…cold as all get out in the winter and hot and stuffy and smellier in the summer.

As a matter of fact, it could be downright dangerous to sit on that toilet seat in the winter. The reason? Well, everyone knows that a boy can toss a horseshoe and have it land right around that stake for a ringer; they can hit a target with a spitball from 20 feet away; and they can knock a moving chipmunk off a wall with a BB gun from a fair distance. I have never figured out why, with all this wonderful hand/eye coordination they seem to possess, they are unable to hit an open hole the size of a large dinner plate when they are holding the weapon (filled with liquid and ready to shoot) just a few inches above the hole. The fact is, though, that many times they cannot, and the result of a miss is a wet toilet seat…and the result of a wet seat in a Townsend Harbor winter is an icy toilet seat. This is why it could be downright dangerous (and at the very least, uncomfortable) to sit on this seat in the winter.

Now, our toilet was not an "outhouse" in the usual sense of the word. A real outhouse is an outside building away from the house. Ours was away from the living quarters but not outside and "down the path" from the house. If you went out the door that was next to the kitchen sink, you would enter a long narrow shed. Just as you entered the shed from the kitchen, on your right hung a large burlap bag. This was the bag that we used to throw old tin cans in. (We had separation of paper, garbage and metal even in those days.) The can bag, however, is something I will get back to in a later story.

If you walked about eight more feet past the can bag, on your left would be the back stairs that my father and the boys used each morning to come downstairs. If you continued on, straight ahead about another six feet, or so, you would be at the toilet door.

Upon opening that door, you would see a built-in, bench-type seat with two holes in it. I have never figured out what type of person might have come up with the idea, or why two-holers were invented. (And I understand there were even <u>three-holers</u> in some places.) I, for the life of me, can not picture two adults sitting side by side, doing their personal business...much less three people. I know I have no memory of seeing two adults in the toilet at the same time. I guess, however, if they were in there at the same time, the door would have been closed, and it is not something they would discuss or advertise to others anyway.

I do know that the toilet did, at times, accommodate two little girls. Kids are so great when they are still young enough not to have acquired modesty. To kids, the matter of moving your bowels is just as un-embarrassing as brushing your hair in front of someone.

I can remember a few times, Joey and I sitting side-by-side on the two-holer, sharing and discussing the pictures in A *Ladies Home Journal* magazine, or maybe it was a *Women's Home Companion*. At any rate, it was one of those magazines that had all the great pictures. We would take the magazine, go into the toilet, pull down our britches and climb up on the seat. There, side-by-side, as we answered the call of nature, we very matter-of-factly chatted about the clothes and food in the book. I don't know how old we were then... probably around four for Joey and six for me. I know it was before I could read much beyond "See Spot Run."

The other great thing about the toilet was that no one, and I mean no one, ever disturbed you there. We could be in there for a very long time, and nobody would call and ask, "What are you two doing now?" because there really wasn't anything you could do in the toilet except what it was intended for. In a house with a family as big as ours, finding a place where no one would bother you was a real accomplishment and, as I think back, that was probably the only place that total privacy was available.

When I found my first love...Larry...on one of my summer trips to Providence, R.I., he and I would exchange letters after my vacation was over and I returned home. I was probably 12 or 13 at the time. I used to take his letters out to the toilet to read them. Not a very romantic place, I admit, and the thought brings a chuckle to me as I write it.

Larry was a fine Jewish boy from a fine Jewish family. He grew up to be a successful lawyer, I understand, and according to Joey, who lived in R.I., he was quite involved in R.I. politics. She has sent me a couple of clippings from local newspapers testifying to this. But, no matter who he was or what he became, even if President of the U.S., his love letters to me had been read in our toilet.

So, I didn't mind the hot/smelly, cold/icy-seated toilet. I didn't know anything else and really never gave it much thought. It was "just the way it was" and I accepted it. The only time I hated it was when it was dark and I had the urge. We would be sitting in the living room, listening to the radio and I would hold it as long as I could, but finally would have to say to my mother, "I have to go to the toilet. Will you come with me?" And she would go with me, out through the shed (which was lighted with a single small, overhead bulb, but scary to me) and stand and wait while I did my business.

It was especially scary on Sunday nights because that was the night that the program "*Inner Sanctum Mysteries*" was on, and it started with a creepy voice saying, "*Welcome. Enter through the creaking door of the inner sanctum,*" and you would hear a door eerily squeaking before they began their scary story about someone being killed or about some other weird thing. Our toilet door creaked! Need I say more?

INSTILLING THE WORK ETHIC

It probably seems by now that life was just fun and games, growing up in those years in a small town. We did have fun and, for the most part, I have chosen to be selective in documenting my memories. I prefer to dwell on and share happy thoughts, as opposed to sad ones.

Being the youngest of the family had its advantages. I was able to spend more time with my mother in one-on-one situations, because, unlike my older sisters, there were no babies for me to help care for. I especially spent time with her in the kitchen, and although at the time I didn't realize it, I learned a great deal from her.

Though we had lots of laughs and lots of fun, there were equal amounts of hard work for everyone. My older siblings will tell you that I, as the "baby," never did anything. It is true that I didn't have it as hard as some of the older brothers and sisters, but I still did a share of the work. Everyone had responsibilities at home, and while these were not necessarily "set" jobs, you were expected to do what you were told to do when you were told to do it. You did not argue ever with Mickey, and while you might give Maggie an argument, you knew, after a very short while, that it was useless. She was a young woman who grew up in the city (or suburbs) and was brought to the country with four kids (and probably another on the way). She started with no knowledge of gardening or preserving food, much less how to raise and kill chickens, pluck and clean them, and then cook them for an ever-growing family. Thus, she was instrumental in instilling the work ethic in all of us.

I am not sure if the "work ethic" is something that is carried in our genes or if it is taught. I do know, however, that all of my children and grandchildren are hard workers and take great pride in doing a job well. "If you have to dig ditches, that's okay… just be sure it's a good ditch." Words to be passed on. And my husband and I did pass that on.

The baking part was easy for Mom, and seemed to just come naturally. Then again, she used to say she "practically grew up in a bakery," but raising cows and chickens, making your own butter, and rendering the fat from the pig to make lard… all <u>that</u> is all a long way from a city bakery!

But I'm wandering again. It's easy to do when I think of Maggie. As I said before, I have never met a person whom I have admired more than I admired her.

Back to the chores! The four oldest girls probably had it the worst in terms of work because there was always a new baby on the way, and they had to help with the little ones, as well as help with the housework, the gardens, and the animals. Charlotte's job was to milk the cow, and she was the "main milker" for many years. We all might have milked at one time or another, or at least tried our hand at it. I'm not sure, but I do know Charlotte was the main one. Charlotte also liked to clean (and still does), but it must have seemed like a totally thankless job with so many younger ones around to mess it up as soon as she finished cleaning.

The two oldest boys, Larry and Pat, were pretty much in charge of the woodpile, I am told. This meant cutting and splitting it, and then tossing it in the woodshed, which was at the very back of the house. They were supposedly responsible for carrying it in for the stoves, but I am sure my mother carried her share of wood in as well. These jobs were handed down to the younger brothers and sisters as the older ones went to work or got married. Jim and Chuck took over the woodpile and feeding and watering the animals. Larry had inherited the cow-milking job, but when he left, Jim took over that job. Helen and Jean were responsible for helping with the housework and did their fair share of babysitting with me. Nobody escaped the garden!

At some time, Mickey must have carried in a lot of wood, as well as split it, especially when the boys were young, but I have no memory of that ever happening. It's a case of not being able to picture a person doing something that you have never seen him do.

In my mind, Mickey belonged in the garden, working at the mill, or building or repairing things. I can even see him putting new soles or heels on our shoes… but not carrying in wood. Neither can I picture him milking the cow, feeding the chickens, or even shoveling snow, but I know he must have had to do all those things at some point in time… probably before I was born. Someone surely had to do them and I doubt, that with four or five kids less than nine years old, my mother was able to take on all of these tasks, as well as all the household chores, and still have time to entertain what was frequently a houseful of relatives on a Sunday. Plus, she seldom had more than a year that she wasn't pregnant while still carrying a young one on her hip or suckling at her breast.

There were three gardens, and everyone had to work in the gardens. Even I was unable to escape that, in spite of what the older siblings say. The gardens were not little gardens. The smallest one had only peas planted in it, but it takes a lot of peas to feed a big family like ours for the whole winter, and that is how many peas were planted in that "smallest" garden. The pea garden alone was much bigger than any vegetable garden I have ever planted, that's for sure. The big gardens contained nearly every conceivable vegetable that could be canned, as well as root vegetables that could be stored for winter. All of this food was stored in the cellar all winter. It was nearly as good as going to the grocery store, but one hundred times scarier and much less exciting, since you went to the cellar at least once a day to "bring up" something for supper. If you went to the grocery store once a week, it was a lot.

One job I had was to thin the onion plants. Doesn't sound like such a bad job, and probably it wouldn't have been if my father had planted shorter rows. I think I got that job because I was closest to the ground to start with. It wasn't so far for me to reach down. I remember wishing he would plant ten short rows instead of two very long ones. You would go along pulling up any onions that were crowded together. Sometimes that meant pulling every other onion out of the ground to make sure the others had enough room to grow nice and fat and round. A pretty mindless job that gave you much time to just think. What did I think while I was pulling what seemed like thousands of onions out of the ground? One thought was "It's too hot in the sun to be doing this!" Another was, "Why doesn't he just plant half as many onions and put them farther apart…then I wouldn't have to thin them." And still another, "I am never, ever going to get to the end of this row." I did, every summer, get to the end of the row, and of course came to understand that planting more and thinning later was the best way to assure that you got an adequate yield, because not all the "onion sets" necessarily take root and grow. No matter what the reason, it was a lousy job.

Planting the potatoes was a job, also, that even the youngest ones could handle. My father would take the potatoes that had lots of "eyes "that were left in the potato bin , and he would cut them into pieces. Each piece had to have an eye (the little white sprouts that grow out of potatoes when they get older) in it. He would give us a bucket and a stick about 10" long, and down to the garden we would go. We would place a potato piece, place the stick next to it in the row, place another potato piece at the end, and so on. Doing it this way, the potatoes would all be spaced exactly the same. I didn't mind doing that job.

My father was very particular about his garden. A piece in the local paper once said "I drove by Mickey Conner's house today. He was out in the garden…I think he was waiting and watching for a weed to sprout so that he could pull it out immediately." Mickey had one of the nicest, neatest gardens I have seen.

THE ABOMINABLE CELLAR

I know that I started writing about chores, but I just thought of the cellar and I have to tell you about that! When I think of it now, the cellar (it would probably be called a "basement" today) was a really neat place. I am not kidding when I say it was scary, because to me it really was, but that was when I was a little kid. To tell the truth, it was scary even when I was in high school, but by that time I was "cool," too cool to let anyone know I was scared. I never told anyone I was scared of the cellar. It didn't matter if you were scared or not, anyway… when you were sent down to the cellar to bring up some food, you just went.

The cellar, unlike the toilet, at least had a light in it, but it had so many nooks and crannies and dark spots that the light really didn't do a lot of good. I think it was just a single light bulb hanging from the ceiling. You would flick on the light switch from the top of the stairs and then begin your descent into the damp, cool, shadowy, cobwebby cellar.

I remember hearing the request from Mom to, "go down cellar and get a jar of beans" (or beets, corn, pickles, tomatoes or any of a dozen things). Now, I didn't want to go down to get anything, but if I had to go for something, the jars were the best thing to have to get because that only required opening the door from the kitchen, turning on the light and carefully descending the cellar stairs… never putting your hand out on your left side to hold onto the wall. That wall was made of big bumpy stones, and I was sure (even though the cracks were filled in with cement or something), there was some creature, waiting there to grab my little hand or bite my finger. Worst of all, it might wiggle and squirm with its many-legged little body, trying to get out from under the trap of my flat hand.

So, I would kind of balance my way down the narrow steps, trying hard not to touch the wall. When I would reach the bottom (which was a floor of dirt), without looking left or right, I would quickly run to the many shelves that held the vegetables and fruit. I would then grab whatever I needed, turn, and once again, looking straight ahead, run for the stairs and head up to the kitchen before any of those nasty things that I believed lived down there could grab me. I never looked right or left because I knew that if they saw me looking at them, then they would know that I knew they were there.

I was never really sure if it would be better to pound your feet on the stairs and sing out at the top of your lungs while descending (hoping that might scare all the creatures into their hiding places), or if I should go very quietly (then they would not hear me coming, so would not come out to see what it was). It was a dilemma every time, so I alternated between being noisy and quiet, so they wouldn't get used to one way or the other.

Sometimes, I would try to stomp and use a voice that I thought sounded like my father because I knew they were afraid of him! They never came out. I guess alternating between being loud and quiet must have worked by confusing them.

If my mother said, "Ally, go down and get a jar of beans," I would try to be well on my way before she could add the dreaded words *"and bring up some carrots."* God, how I hated to have to get carrots!!! You see, unlike most of the veggies and fruits, the carrots were not in jars. When the carrots were dug up from the garden in the fall, they would be brought up by the bushel from the garden. The green tops would be cut back (leaving just a couple of inches of the greens), and then the carrots would be brought down to the cellar. On one side of the cellar, there was an opening in the wall, sort of like a small cave about two or three feet wide and about two feet high. At least I think it was about that size. I don't know how far back it went because I never felt or even *looked* inside it. My father would put sand in this little cave, and then he would bury the carrots in the sand to keep them for the winter.

They always *said* that there were just carrots and sand in there and that it was a nice clean little cave, but I was not fooled for one minute! I knew that *any* and *all* kinds of creatures lived in that cave. I also knew that some of these things had stringy cold hair growing out of them because one time, when I had reached in, I *felt it.*

They tried to tell me that it was just the carrot greens sending out new sprouts, but I knew they were lying. I had seen and felt carrot greens when they came up from the garden and they didn't feel anything like that! Besides that, my father always told me that things had to have sun to grow and there was no sun or even any *light* in that hole. I knew that the only things that could grow in there were ugly shriveled things with cold wet, stringy hair growing out of them. I also knew that they were shriveled because I *felt* one like that one time… not just the hair, but a something that was cold and kind of bendy and shrivelly, like maybe a big nose.

I *hated* to get carrots, but if I *had* to, I would go down the stairs and turn toward the carrot bin and slowly put my hand out. My skin would get all bumpy and my stomach would feel like it had left my body and there was just an empty hole there. Then I would hope and pray that I would touch a carrot when I put my hand into that sand, and not one of those creepy, stringy-haired things with the shriveled, bendy nose or finger or whatever it was. I really knew there were whole families of these things living in the carrot bin. I was sure there were little ones that probably didn't have hair yet, and many older mother and father ones with hair, but I know the one I touched was at least the great-grandfather.

So… on one side of the cellar were the shelves stacked nearly to the ceiling with the jars of canned food, and near those shelves was a potato bin, which was just a large box that was open on top and built up on legs to keep the potatoes off the ground. If they got damp they would get rotten and spoiled. Straight in front of you was the coal bin (it seems like everything was called a "bin"), and just above that was a little window so when the man brought coal, he would just back his truck up outside close to the window, and put a little chute through the window and into the cellar. It worked pretty neat. He could dump the coal right down the chute onto the cellar floor, and it would keep coming and coming until there was a humongous pile reaching almost to the ceiling. And what a loud racket it would make when that coal was being dumped in!

On the other wall was the dreaded carrot bin, and hanging from the beams above were cabbages and turnips. The turnips were kind of fun. When they were dug up from the garden and brought to the house to be stored for winter, my mom would heat a big kettle of paraffin wax. She would clean the turnips all off, and then she would dip them into the warm, melted paraffin to coat them to keep them from spoiling. Then, when they were hard and dry, they would have a piece of twine wrapped around them and be hung from the beams in the cellar. I liked them because they were hard, and shiny, and safe looking, without anything covering them up. Sometimes I would look at them in the dim light and think maybe they were the heads of a bunch of little bald men.

The cabbages didn't need any wax or anything. They were just pulled up from the garden, and my mom would tie string around their roots and they would be hung upside down too. They were kind of scary! They had big leaves, and I sometimes used to wonder if maybe there were real heads inside all of those big floppy green leaves. If one was hanging low, I would duck and try to avoid touching it because if there was a head inside there, I didn't want to feel it… plus, I could just imagine what it's face would look like after hanging upside down in the dark cellar for days or weeks or months. I was taking no chances. If I had to get a cabbage, I would climb on the little wooden box that was there, and without touching the cabbage, unhook the whole string off the nail that held it, and carry it upstairs, holding it out as far away from my body as I could.

I would put the cabbage on the metal cooking table in the kitchen and leave it for someone else (usually my mother) to peel off those big leaves and expose what I thought might be a gray, shriveled shrunken head and face. I knew that if my mother peeled off the leaves, it would look just like a cabbage, but if I did it, it just might be one of those ugly heads!

As I said before, I took no chances when it came to things from the cellar.

THE WOODSHED AND BEYOND

There was no meat in the cellar, ever. Meat was, for the most part, stored in the shed or the woodshed. The woodshed was rather interesting, and, at times, a fun place. It was not scary like the cellar. It was especially fun in the late fall. We would go out there and see, hanging on ropes, tied to the beams, big hams and slabs of bacon that were sometimes as long as the pig they were taken from. There would be smoked hams and fresh hams, too.

I loved to go out there just after the pork got back from the smokehouse, because it smelled so good. In the fall, the wood was sometimes piled nearly to the ceiling, so we could play "King of the Mountain," if my mother didn't know we were playing out there. It wasn't very safe climbing on loose piles of wood that way.

More of the meat was in the shed that was attached to the woodshed. There was a big wooden barrel that was filled with "rock salt," rather like the stuff they put on icy roads, only clean. Some of the pork would be kept in that barrel with the rock salt and water. This was called "salt pork," and it tasted really good when Mom baked beans with the salt pork in them. Salt pork was also used in the base for fish chowder or corn chowder and other tasty stuff.

Occasionally, when going barefoot in the summer, someone

would step on a nail that was in the yard. If this happened, my mother would clean the puncture wound with yellow soap and water; she would then take a small slice of salt pork and place it on the bottom of the foot, covering the wound, and secure it tightly with tape or bandage strips, wrapped around the foot. When you were out and about, other kids would look and say, "Stepped on a nail, huh?" After wearing the salt pork for a day or so, you would wake up in the middle of the night and it would feel like there was a giant suction cup pulling on the bottom of your foot. That was when, supposedly, the salt pork had "done its job and drawn all the poison out of the wound." Then it was safe to take the salt pork off your foot. I don't know if that really was a cure or if we were just lucky, but we never got tetanus or an infected foot with this method. I wouldn't suggest trying it, but I wouldn't try a lot of the old "home remedies" that were used in those days...like cooking the fat out of the chicken skins and mixing it with dry mustard to make a salve, to rub on your chest when you had a bad chest cold.

There was also another kind of barrel in the shed with pickling juice in it. This barrel held pickled pigs feet; I loved those things, and still do, although it is nearly impossible to find them anymore. Along with the wooden barrels was a big metal barrel in the shed where the corn (I think for the chickens) was kept.

I remember one time a rat got into that barrel and was eating the corn or grain. My brother decided that the best way to take care of that was to put our cat in the barrel, and she would kill the rat. He dropped the cat into the barrel, and we heard a bit of yowling and scurrying and squeaking and then...out came the cat! He tried a second time, but the cat was smarter than my brother and jumped out immediately.

My father came on the scene and took the metal cover, put it on the barrel, grabbed the sledgehammer, and slammed it against the side of the barrel. He then took the top off, and the rat was deader than a doornail. I was not at all familiar with cartoons at that time, but I now have a picture in my mind of what happened to that rat when the hammer hit the barrel… it would make a great cartoon: One of those BO-I-I-I-N-N-G cartoons with everything vibrating. And in the next picture you would see a cross-eyed rat lying… dead.

HIGH SHOES AND BLOOMERS

The shoes that I usually got in the wintertime served two purposes. They were used as inside and outside shoes. I imagine it was cheaper to buy one pair of what we called "snow boots" or "snow shoes" than to buy a pair of shoes and a pair of rubber boots to go over them, so snow boots it was for me. How I hated those things! They were like the high shoes that I wear much of the winter now, but it seemed to me that I was the only kid in the school that had them, and I thought they were ugly.

These boots came up over the ankle and were usually lined with sheepskin and a little bit of the lining turned down over the top, like a collar. I usually got brown (a color I really hated), but once in a while I could talk my mother into buying white ones for me. I didn't like the white ones either, but they were a little more feminine and more tolerable than the brown or black.

Thinking back, I must have been quite a sight going off to school in the late fall. I would have to wear "bloomers" and long brown cotton stockings or knee socks (on warmer days) with those high-top shoes and a dress. The only thing I hated more than high-top shoes was bloomers! I don't know if you know what bloomers are, but the only way I can describe them is to say that if you took a pair of your longest, baggiest shorts that were made of flannel and put elastic on the legs and waist so that they ballooned out between the waist and the legs, you would have a pair of bloomers. I think they should have been called "balloonmers" because that is what they looked like. And on me, with my toothpick legs and knobby knees hanging out from under, it must have been a real sight. The bloomers usually came just above the knee, and my dress was about the same length so… picture it!

We had to walk a short way (maybe equivalent to a short block) to the corner where we caught the bus for school. I would, on the "bloomer" mornings, dally until my brothers had gone to the bus stop, and then I would amble up the street until I came to a parked car to hide behind. Sometimes a fat tree would have to do if no cars were available. I would hide behind whatever object I could find, and I would pull the legs of my bloomers up as high under my skirt as I could so that they wouldn't show beneath my dress.

I know now that this must have looked even funnier, because the bloomers must have made a big balloon bunch near the tops of my legs and make my skirt bulge out, but I didn't know that then. I only knew that no one could see my bloomers. Little Ally, off to school with her wispy, white-blonde hair, her skinny little body in her little dress with the big bunch all the way around. This was all being transported on knobby-kneed toothpicks that were covered in stockings that were the same color as the brown lunch bag I carried. And to top it all off, I was very pigeon-toed at that time. As you know, my brothers called me "Ding-toed Ally." As I see this child (in my mind's eye), I am surprised that that was the worst they called me.

But love is blind, and I knew I was loved. My sisters thought I was cute.

MUSICAL MOUSETRAP

The "Victrola" lived in the back room… a small room off the kitchen. Most of you younger than I am, probably have no idea what a Victrola is. The truth is if there had been no Victrola, there probably would not have been stereos, tape players, and disc players, along with the other various electronic gizmos we have today. The Victrola was the father of them all, and what a wonderful surprise it was when we got ours!

Once again, I think someone gave it to us. It must seem like we never bought anything: the fact of the matter is, we only bought the necessities in those days. Necessities meant clothes, food, and fuel, (which was wood, coal and oil for the living room and kitchen stoves). Beyond that, of course, necessities included blankets and sheets, medicines, etc., but there was no room in the budget for music other than what was given to us and what we made ourselves. One of the things we could make was a musical comb. We would just take a regular comb and wrap a piece of waxed paper around it. Then if you just close your lips around it and hum, it vibrates and make great music. I was visiting at my friend, Dolores Boucher's house in California a couple of years ago. She had never played a comb so we got a couple of combs out and I taught her how to do it. We had a lot of laughs over that one. Two elderly ladies, entertaining themselves making music with waxed paper wrapped combs. What a sight!

But, back to the Victrola. The Victrola was a type of record player. The one we had resembled a tall cabinet that stood about four feet high, and had a hinged cover on top. When you lifted the cover, you would see a turntable and an "arm" that held the needle. You would put the record on the turntable, and before you started the record, you would have to crank a handle on the side of the cabinet to wind up the spring… rather like a wind-up music box or toy. It was not electric, and so would not play unless it was wound up. After winding it up by the crank, you would pick up the arm and move it over so that the needle rested on the record. The next step was to push a little lever on the side of the turntable, and the record would start playing.

The funny thing (and we thought it was the fun thing about the Victrola) was that when it first started playing, it would start off really slow, and then go faster and faster until it got to a normal speed. Then it would run at normal speed for a while, but as the tightened spring wound down, it would go slower and s-l-o-w-e-r until finally it would stop until you wound it up again. If you wound it while it was still turned to the "on" setting, it was especially funny, because the singer would go from v-e-r-y-s-l-o-w to very, very fast and would always create giggles from the kids and usually a comment from any adult who was within hearing range. We didn't, as I have noted before, have much, but we did know how to laugh and to create our own entertainment. The sky was the limit when it came to imagination.

Fun with the VIctrola, and creating you own entertainment in the back room, reminds me of another situation that occurred and gave us several days of fun (and many giggles) by the piano. This was musical entertainment in a way, but it was created by a mouse.

We discovered there was a mouse in the piano. The younger Conner kids quickly found that, after some experimentation, we could make that mouse go from one side of the piano to the other. Of course, he probably spent more time inside the piano just pigging out on the felt covering the little hammers that made the notes play. I still picture what it must have been like for him… a little field mouse. He found his way into a warm house as winter was approaching and food was getting scarce. When he made his way inside the piano, it must have seemed made to order as a winter home: a nice big box, where he was warm and protected, lots of space for exercising, and all of those nice pieces of felt material on sticks, sitting nicely in a row like deformed lollipops served buffet style, and lined up for a winter of feasting. The felt on the hammers must have been held together by glue, or something that was tasty to mice.

The only thing lacking was a dish of water, he probably thought, for there was certainly adequate sleeping space. "Oh well," he might have figured (if mice can figure), " it's still pretty nice. The cat can't get me in here; it's warm, plenty of food, and I can just run out to the kitchen at night when the cat is sleeping and fill up on water… this felt is filling, and it makes you pretty thirsty." Well, that mouse had a few days of living the good life before the Conner kids discovered him. We found that if we played the low notes on the left side of the piano, we could make him run, scampering and squeaking, to the far right side of the piano. He certainly did squeak loudly. The piano notes must have sounded like cymbals crashing in his poor little ears. Then, when we got him over to the right side of the piano, we would play the high notes and send him squeaking in protest back toward the low notes.

Sometimes, we would quickly play a note in the middle of the keyboard, and he would stop and head back to the high notes again, only to be turned around by the loud plink of a high note just before he got to the end. I think now of that poor little mouse… We didn't regard it as torturing the thing. He only lasted a few days, and then he either found his way out and decided to take his chances with the cold, or died of a heart attack from running 100 mouse miles two or three times a day, back and forth inside the piano. He probably went completely deaf, too.

He must have left, because we never smelled his decaying body in the back room. If he had died in there, the piano probably would have played, but the fumes would have certainly discouraged anyone from getting close to it, at least for a while.

I like to consider it not as torturing the mouse, but saving the piano. There was no way we knew of that could have gotten the mouse out of there except to "chase" him out with our playing. And, if he had stayed, he certainly would have done a major job on those felt covers before winter was over. Worse yet, what if it were a pregnant female?

ADDENDUM TO "MUSICAL MOUSETRAP"

After Doug Cooper, my editor, read the "Musical Mousetrap" story, he sent me an e-mail that said, "Alice, what do you think happened to that mouse, and what if it was a pregnant female? I think it would be interesting to hear what you think the outcome was. Why don't you add an ending to this story?" Without pondering the question for more than a minute, I wrote back to him… "You asked for it, Doug, here it is," and immediately typed and sent out this reply:

If it were indeed, a pregnant female, I could imagine in my childish mind's eye, that female sinking into a nest of dusty cobwebs lined with softly chewed felt and bearing nine tiny hairless little pink mice. She wouldn't hear when they were complaining because she had lost her hearing weeks ago after she moved into this piano.

These mice grew and began to roam around their big-box home, learning to eat the felt from the hammers, a food that was quite tasty, but for more nourishment, their mother would sneak out at night and steal some of the cat's or dog's food from their dishes and bring it back to them.

Occasionally, someone would come in and start banging on the piano keys which, eventually, destroyed the babies' hearing also. Getting bigger and hungrier, they began, however, to forage outside the piano box on their own. They were fat, very fat, and deaf…very deaf…and so… did not hear the cat coming. She snacked on one or two mice daily until they were all gone, and the cat got fatter and fatter.

I don't know what happened to that mother mouse. I think she went out looking for the lost children. She may have joined her little ones. She was never seen again. The fat cat slowly returned to normal size.

The moral of the story is…"Do not ask Alice to end a story when she has no ending in her brain."

MOM'S HANDS

I remember Mom's hands. Sometimes I look at my own hands now and am reminded of hers. Her fingers were not as thin (and bony) as mine, but she had many wrinkles and arthritic bumps on her hands. It's funny because as I look at my own knobby fingers, almost always stiff and sometimes painful with arthritis, I think of how ugly they are. Yet, I always remember loving my mother's hands and not ever noticing that they were swollen or knobby. At least, not until I was out of my teens.

I would stand by her when she played the piano, and honestly think her hands had magic. They could, it seemed, do anything. She played the piano well, although she couldn't read a musical note. As I said earlier, I was told that in her younger years, that when they only had silent movies, she played the musical accompaniment for one of the movie houses in the Boston area. This is another one of those stories that one or some of the older sisters told. It is another story that I am not sure is accurate, but having watched her play when I was growing up, it certainly is very believable.

The piano in our house was an extremely important piece of furniture. It wasn't any fancy type of piano, just an old upright, and I am sure that it was given to us, but it was a focal point for most, if not all, of the family.

It was not uncommon to have a group of my parents' friends or relatives at our house. It seemed we would invariably end up around the piano with my mother playing the old songs and all of us standing around her, singing. The piano was not in the living room, but had been placed in the little room off the kitchen that was called simply "the back room." That was the same room that housed the Victrola I spoke about earlier. That room was very small. As I remember, it probably measured 8'x10' or a little larger. In fact, once the piano was in there, a minimal amount of space was left for anything else.

I don't remember any other furniture being in that room except for the piano and the Victrola. I could try to be classy and say that it was the "music room" or the "family room," but why pretend? It was the "back room" to all. That old back room housed some of the truly great family times for the Conner kids and their friends and relatives. That back room was where I was introduced to my first piano when I was four or five years old. It was where I played my first notes and found that, while I was not great at playing the piano, it gave me tremendous pleasure… and an outlet for my emotions. When I was glad, I played happy songs; mad, banging songs; or sad, melancholy songs. The old piano was, at times, my best friend and was always there if I needed company. The piano that I have now, and have had for many years, is the same way. I cannot imagine being without a piano.

I recognized, many years ago, that I will never become a "pianist," but I also found over the years that wherever there is a piano, there is a good time. People really don't care that you play <u>well</u>. They only care that you can play the songs they want to sing, and I was fortunate enough to have inherited some of my mother's talent and "ear for music." If I have heard a song, I can usually play it. I am not saying that I can play it exactly the way it was written, but I can at least play it well enough that it is recognizable… and that seems to amaze a lot of people.

People still say to me, on occasion, "How do you know where to put your fingers?" My answer has never changed, "I don't know… my fingers just seem to know where to go." It is something that I can't explain. Sometimes lately, I feel very sad because the piano I now have is dying a slow death. It will no longer hold a tuning for long and it has an occasional "sticky key". I wonder whether, when this piano goes, I will get another one. I will nurse it as long as I can. It is rather scary and sad for me to think of myself without a piano.

When I got older, the old piano accompanied brother Chuck and me as we prepared and practiced for our roles in various operettas and musicals in high school. It accompanied brother Larry and me as we sang duets and played piano duets, and as I have said before, it was the center of many gatherings at our house.

When I got married in 1952 and moved away, the same old piano was still in the same place in the back room. Mice had eaten some of the felts and it was out of tune and a bit tinny-sounding. On the night before I got married a group of us was around the piano singing while I played. That was in February. The following summer, my husband, Fred, and I came home to spend a weekend. We pulled into the yard, and I couldn't believe my eyes. My piano (and by that time I thought of it as my piano (even though most of the family had played it at some time) was being cut up and tossed out the back room window, in pieces! I sat and watched for a few minutes and became very teary-eyed. The piano had played its last song. The easiest way to get it out of the room was in pieces, and so that is how it went out. Fred, seeing my distress, put his arm around me and said, "Don't cry, Honey, I'll get you another piano someday." He still had another year of college left, at least, and intellectually I knew he did not have the money to buy, of all things, a piano. I believed him anyway. I knew that someday I would have my own piano in my own house.

I went for a lot of years without a piano after that…about seven or eight years… until I finally got another old upright. When that upright died many years later, my oldest son, Larry, made me a pair of earrings with the ivory keys. He scrimshawed a design in them for me and they are something else that I treasure. I have not been without a piano since then, and I hope I never have to be without one again. The grandchildren have enjoyed it as much as I, and the piano in my house is as much of a focal point when the grandchildren are visiting, as the old piano was in the "back room" when I was growing up. I especially enjoy when granddaughter, Angie, (a talented musician and music major) and I sit and play duets.

PENNED PLAYMATES

Besides ham and beef, a Conner mainstay was chicken. Since we raised our own, it could be counted on fairly frequently for dinner. I think chickens are among the dumbest and funniest creatures ever created. There is no way you can imagine what I am about to tell you. You would have to sit and watch chickens for a long time.

General rules for chickens seem to be that the other guy always has the best thing to peck at, and you can usually be sure that, to their pea-sized brains, the last thing to be thrown to them is what they always think is the best thing. We would make a game out of trying to pick which chicken was the smartest by choosing the one that each of us thought would be the least likely to follow the pack; i.e., the smartest, in our minds. We would bet matchsticks or marbles. Sometimes we would even bet something quite valuable like a Big-Little Book or a comic book.

Anyway, we would choose our chicken, and then one of us would throw a piece of food into the pen, which held a dozen or more chickens. Naturally, they would all rush squawking to grab the piece of food. Then, while they were all fighting over the food, we would throw something inedible into the pen. It might be a colored stone, a bright leaf, or even a button… almost anything would do. As soon as one of them spotted the stone or leaf, she would leave the food pack and run toward the object that was last thrown in the pen. Sure enough, they would all leave the food and turn to chase after her, thinking that whatever the other hen was after must be better than what they had. This game could go on for long periods of time, depending on how long our attention span was and/or how quickly we might come up with some other, more entertaining idea, like giving bubble gum to the pigs.

If you have a big (and I mean double big) wad of bubble gum and throw it in to a pig, he will get it in his mouth and when he starts to chew, it gets stringy and sticks to his teeth. A pig would sometimes try chewing it for what seemed like minutes and end up with a whole lot of gloppy, stringy bubble gum in his mouth. They don't usually try to spit it out or anything. It was pretty funny to watch. Come to think of it, I don't know if I ever saw a pig spit anything out. They just eat. You think maybe they don't know how to spit?

ADDENDUM TO "PENNED PLAYMATES"

Once again, Doug, my editor, has sent me an e-mail asking me how I think the chickens and pigs really felt when we played these tricks on them. (I'm wondering if he's taking a course in animal psychiatry or something.) Anyway, I gave it very little thought and then decided I would answer his question. I've observed both chicken and pigs over the years, so feel somewhat qualified and confident in my answer.

I rather think that these animals and fowl enjoyed seeing us kids visit occasionally. It must have broken up their long, monotonous day. For the chickens, all they did was walk around the chicken coop from dawn to sunset (except for the rooster, and he would "strut.") looking for pieces of grain or corn that someone else had missed. No stimulation whatsoever until we arrived with our little pockets full of "chick tricks." Bright marbles or stones, even if they weren't edible, must have set some kind of electrical current buzzing in their pea brains. I like to think that they were laughing and maybe giggling at the foolishness of the game, much like children would when playing "hide the pea."

The pigs, however, I am sure enjoyed the bubble gum. Especially Bernice. I named every sow (female pig) that we had, Bernice. "Bernice's bacon is really good," I might say at the breakfast table, long after Bernice had been slaughtered for food and another Bernice had taken her place in the pen. She would come over, snorting and grunting, when we approached the fence. Pigs just loved to be scratched behind the ears, almost as much as they loved food, so we would occasionally get a small stick, reach in and scratch them behind the ears, and then give them bubble gum. You should try it someday. They will sidle right up to the fence and once you start rubbing them, they don't want you to stop. They are really sweet animals. It's just that no one ever gives them a chance. I know the gum was sticky in their mouths, but at least it was sweet. Come to think of it though, I'm not sure if pigs even have taste buds. I never saw one of them refuse food, no matter how bad it looked, smelled, or tasted. So, maybe they loved seeing us come!

At least our visits to the animals must have been an occasional break in their otherwise boring existence.

PART III
GROWING UP IN THE HARBOR

THE HARBOR

Let me tell you just a little bit about the village where I grew up. Townsend, Massachusetts, is a town comprised of three small villages… Townsend Center, Townsend Harbor, and West Townsend. The town was, in the 30s and 40s, a factory town or "mill town" with the leather-board factory in The Harbor and lumber mills in The Center and West Townsend. The town is situated about forty miles northwest of Boston, or as natives would say, "fawty miles nawth" of Boston. My growing-up years were spent in the village of Townsend Harbor, generally known as "The Harbor." The other two sections of the town were most often referred to, by locals, as "The Center" and "West Townsend."

The Harbor was a nice place to grow up, and while many of the houses in The Center and West Townsend were larger, and in some cases grander, I don't remember wishing or wanting to live in any other section of town. I am sure that I wished to live in a grander house. Most children do wish for that.

The street I lived on was the main road in the village. Travelers also knew it as Route 119, but to us it was just Main Street, aptly named, as it was the main street in the village. Our house was the first one you would come to as you entered the village if you were driving northwest on Route 119 toward New Hampshire, the border of which was only about three or four miles from The Harbor. Across from our house was the leatherboard factory where my father worked. No long commute for him, that's for sure. Less than a one-minute walk across the street, and he was there.

Our little village didn't have a center in the literal sense of the word. There was a crossroad a short way up the street from our house, and I truly do not remember anyone ever calling those roads by name. If you turned right you were going "up the hill" or "up the back road" and left was just "over the bridge." We did have a post office at the crossroads, and next to that was a fire house and a little beyond the fire house was Leland's Store. This little one-room store in the back of the storeowner's house stocked bread, milk and many other staples… most of which I can't remember. Probably that is because we seldom bought anything at that store except an occasional loaf of bread (my mother baked our own), and once in a great while, when I got a penny, a piece of candy.

Our little village also had a gristmill, where in earlier years the farmers had their grain ground, and a cooperage, where barrels were made. I know the gristmill was not a working mill while I was growing up. In front of the cooperage was a canal. This provided many a happy hour in the summer. It was like having our own swimming pool in addition to the pond. I think the cooperage was operating, but I'm not positive about that. These buildings are now both owned by the Townsend Historical Society. According to my research, the gristmill is still operable but is, as of this writing, closed and under repair. The cooperage is open to the public as an antique shop. In back of these two buildings are the beloved Harbor Pond and the dam, both of which are fed by the Squannicook River. I would like to relate a quick little aside about the name of that river. I don't remember the source of the story, but one time, I asked a man who lived in Townsend Center how the Squannicook got its name. He told me this fabled story: He said that many years ago, the Indians lived along the river, and one day an Indian warrior came back to camp after being gone all day… out with his hunting party. When he got back to his teepee, his wife (squaw) had no dinner prepared for him. He was furious, and went all through the camp telling everyone "Squaw no cook, squaw no cook" and that, according to the legend passed to me, is how the Squannicook got it's name."

As children, the story we were told was that The Harbor was so named because it was a part of the Underground Railroad, and was instrumental in "harboring" the slaves. This story was reinforced in our minds due to the fact that there was a large stone in the wall of the dam that had a date on it. I cannot remember what that date was, but supposedly that stone was removable, and behind it was a tunnel that led under the harbor pond and into the cellar of the old mansion that stood on the other side of the pond, just over the bridge. Whether this story is factual or folklore I have no idea, but it was the story I grew up believing.

Some historians believe that The Harbor was so named because it was a safe harbor from the Indians, and others claim it was because the area was an encampment for soldiers. I do not know which it was, but I like our growing-up version best.

Another store, LeClaire's, was farther up the street. That store had two gas pumps in front, but it also was very small and sold only a few grocery items. The back of this property had a small dock and, I think, rented rowboats when I was young. Across the street from that store was the "Harbor Farm," which was, to the best of my memory, a rather large dairy farm. Those were the main buildings in the village, and in all, I would guess there were possibly 12 to 15 houses on each side of the street to the end of the village.

It was a small and cozy village where everybody knew everybody. If you really wanted to keep a secret, you could not tell anyone! If you told one person, most of the village would know it within a very short period of time, and as it was passed on, the facts might be skewed so that your original secret may not even be recognizable. Gossipy? Of course! Aren't all small towns? There were not a lot of interesting things going on in our town, so when a new tid-bit did get out, it was fair game to grab on to it. It provided some new, exciting topics of conversation.

TRAIN TRACKS

The railroad track was just across the street from our house, and while in this day and age, many people would not buy a house near a railroad track, that track was pretty neat to us. The train would come by twice a day, and we would always know it was coming because we would hear the whistle blowing as it neared the crossing that was just a little way up from the house.

Somehow, accidentally perhaps, the engineer and I started to wave to each other each day, and it soon became evident that he looked forward to waving to the little blonde girl as much as I looked forward to waving to him.

It soon got to be a daily ritual… I would hear the whistle and run out the door and wait on the front lawn for the train to slow down before approaching the crossing. He would spot me, and we would give each other our best waves. The best part came a few weeks into that summer of waving, when one day he slowed down, as usual, and instead of waving, tossed me a Peppermint Patty candy bar. (They were round and flat like a patty.) Every day after that on his trip through, I would get a Peppermint Patty, and <u>then</u> a wave. I think I was around four or five that summer, and it is strange that I still think of him when I see Peppermint Patties.

I don't recall his face... only his striped cap and his black-gloved hand waving and tossing me candy. Candy was a real treat, as we did not often get it, so that was the high point of my day for many days that summer. It makes me realize now, that you don't have to give a lot to kids to make them happy, unless, of course, they have been given so much that they no longer have an appreciation for the little things.

The train track had many purposes for us. They were quite safe because the train came through only twice a day, and almost always at the same time. You knew that you were not to be on the tracks before lunch (the train came through between 11 and 12, I think) and before supper (it came back around 4 or 5 as I remember). However, in between those times, the track was a part of our playground as well as a great route to take if you were "running away from home," or if you were bringing a fresh-cut Christmas tree from out of the woods. Trees could be dragged much more easily on the tracks. The railroad track was the shortest route to the canal for swimming or to the swimming hole.

The track rails themselves were great for learning how to "balance walk." If you used a board to balance walk, you could only go one at a time. On the tracks, you could walk side-by-side, one on each track, or you could line up as many as you wanted. The rails were good for playing "follow the leader," great for "walking with a limp" by walking with one foot on the track and the other on the ground, and besides being useful for cutting an occasional snake in half, the rail was great for flattening coins. We didn't often have a coin that we wanted to waste by flattening it, but occasionally someone would feel rich enough to make the sacrifice. We would lay the coin on the track just before the train came, and after the train passed, we would retrieve this wonderfully flattened coin. I don't know why we wanted flattened coins, but I don't know why people wanted pet rocks 50 years later, either.

Speaking of rocks, someone told us once that if we put a rock on the track that the train would hit it and jump off the track. It doesn't work. We tried it many times. We didn't think of derailing and crashing the train. That never occurred to us. We only thought that the train would jump off the track and just stop, right across the street from our house! What excitement that would be! Every kid in town would be down at our house watching them get the train back on the track. We had no idea how that could be accomplished. We only knew that we would have a train sitting right across the street from our house. We would be celebrities!

I think we sort of thought of it as maybe "capturing" the train, and it would be "our train" because we would be the ones who were smart enough to have been able to get it off the track. I don't think we ever knew the word "derail." Ah, the innocence of children.

And the trestle! Talk about balance walking… the trestle was the best place to do it. For those who don't know what a trestle is, it is a railroad bridge that, in our case anyway, carried the train over the water.

Our trestles weren't very long but no less challenging to a little kid than one that was a half-mile long. The trestle was basically built with logs, called railroad ties, spaced just about wide enough apart so your foot could fit through the space between. On top of these logs, the tracks were laid. It was quite a challenge and a feat to be able to balance walk across the trestle, all the while knowing that if you lost your balance or slipped, you had only a 50/50 chance of <u>not</u> having your foot slip between the railroad ties. If that happened, we just knew that you could be suspended with one leg stuck, up to the hip, between those ties.

I used to imagine that if that happened, the kid would just hang there and if no one came to help before it was time for the train to come, the train would hit him. Then the body would be pushed, one leg attached, up the track on the "cow catcher" on the front of the train, while the other leg would drop into the water and be found floating in the canal by the kids who were swimming there. Of course, no one I know of ever got caught in the trestle, but it was kind of neat and gory to think about. We were not often bored… our imaginations bailed us out of many a potentially boring moment.

SUMMER SHENANIGANS

Summers were filled with free playtime. There were no day camps or organized summer programs. But summer was also a time of work for us. We needed to give to the garden in order for it to give us the vegetables that we would eat all winter. The garden vegetables needed to be weeded, hoed, thinned, picked, and prepared or canned to be stored in the cellar for winter consumption. You probably cannot imagine canning enough of everything - vegetables as well as fruit and pie fillings, to last a family of 10 or 12 people all winter. At that time, many people did just that, but most did not have a family the size of ours. Even in those times, our family was extraordinarily large, but nearly all of our food was homegrown. When the bushels of peas or beans would be brought up from the garden, we would sit on the porch (we called it a piazza… it is rather strange that we would use that word) and take part in snapping the beans or shelling the peas. The peas were probably the worst. It takes a bushel of peas to get just a pot full since there aren't that many peas in each pod. I probably didn't like that job at the time, except for the fact that I love raw vegetables, and so it would be two for the pot, one for my mouth. That was kind of our reward for shelling peas or snapping beans.

Our summers were also filled with swimming at the "swimming

hole," also known as "the Harbor Pond." It was a firm and fast rule that we were not allowed to go swimming before Memorial Day, no matter how hot it got. That was my father's rule. I never really understood it, but my mother never gave permission to do something that my father ruled against, and swimming before Memorial Day fell into that category. We didn't like that, but today, I say, "Hooray for the parents who stick together with their rules!"

We would come home from school in late May and the temperature might be 80 or higher. We would ask and beg my mother to let us go swimming and she, of course, would say, "No." After a while, tired of our begging, she would say, "Go ask your father," and so we would trek across the street, scared stiff to ask, but wanting to go swimming with the rest of the kids in town. They were already there, usually, swinging on a rope tied to a branch of the big tree on the bank, and flying out over the pond and then dropping into the water with a great splash.

Anyway, we would go across the street to the factory where he was working and meekly ask "Papa, can we go swimming?" Usually he would just say, "No," but sometimes he would think for a moment and say, "Alright, go ahead." Other times he would say, "If it's okay with your mother, you can go." If the answer was "Yes," we would come home and quickly don our suits and fly to the pond to join in the fun. If he said "No," we knew there was no use arguing... even if we dared to (which we didn't). So, we would mope away and find something else to do.

I think back now on swimming in the pond. The rope swing was a great source of amusement. Sometimes we would have a big burlap bag stuffed with old rags tied on the end of the rope... that gave us a great "seat." One time we had a tire tied on to the end of the rope and two or three could hang on and all jump off at the same time and create a really big splash. As in most ponds, there were turtles - some quite large, and black water snakes, some, also, quite large.

They never bothered anyone that I know of… they were no more anxious to come near us than we were of going near them, so they usually stayed out nearer the center of the pond, away from the activity. It was not uncommon, though, to come out of the pond and hear someone say, "You've got a bloodsucker on you." I hated those things! They don't hurt, you can't even feel that they are on you, but the idea of that slimy black thing sucking my blood was creepy. Usually, very matter-of-factly, one of the kids would pick it off and fling it in the dirt where it would dry up.

Some of our summer activities were rather weird, and I suspect if my mother knew of some of the things we did, she would have certainly disapproved. We would wait until we heard the train coming and fetch the snake, (just a small one… I don't remember ever catching a big snake) from whatever place we had stashed him, bonk him on the head to knock him out, and lay him on the track. We would then stand back and watch the train run over him. After the train had gone by, we would quickly run back to the tracks to watch both ends of the snake wriggling as if still attached. " Weird kids!" you're probably thinking. I heartily agree with you. That little way of amusing ourselves didn't happen very often, but I do remember doing it a couple of times.

When Joanne would be at our house for vacation time in the summer, she and I would go to the Harbor Pond, get a rowboat, and go out and pick water lilies. We would then set up a "stand" in front of the house in the place where my father would set up a pansy stand in the spring. We would sell water lilies to the people who drove by. A penny a piece for each flower. Since our house was on a main road that was used by many city people going to N.H. and Maine for vacations, we did a pretty good business. Especially on weekends.

Joanne told me a while ago that her husband, Ed, made her a little pond in her back yard and they went to the nursery to buy some water plants for it. They were selling water lilies for $40.00 a plant! Times have changed, for sure. We used to sell them for a penny a piece for the white ones and two cents for the pink ones. Of course, we weren't selling the whole plant, roots and all… just the flowers… but $40.00 for one plant?

UNEXPECTED SUMMER EXCITEMENT

While winter was for homemade skis, summer was a time for stilts. My father would make us stilts out of the scrap lumber that he had left over from some of his carpentry jobs, and we would have a great time with them.

Stilt races were exciting. Sometimes, he would make a pair of stilts with the blocks to place your feet about two feet off the ground, and it was hard to get up on them. If you were really small, you would have somebody hold the stilts until you got up on them, and then you would take off or fall down (depending on whether or not you had learned to balance and walk on them). You always had to learn to walk on the shorter ones first… it was the rule. I learned to walk on the short ones first, but only because it was the only way I would be allowed to get up on the high ones!

The first time I did get on the high ones., I felt like a giant. It was a great sensation. And the bigger, and the better you got at walking on stilts, the longer your stride could be. Stilts are great fun. They were accepted toys for the Conner kids, but I am amazed at how many people who are my age now, never had a chance to try to walk on stilts when they were young. They may have had more money than we did, but they certainly missed out on some of the great things we did because we were poor.

When my grandchildren visited us in Vermont, (I was in my 60s at the time) I brought out stilts that my husband had made for the kids. They were trying to walk on them but just couldn't get the hang of it. I decided that I would have to demonstrate how it was done; rather than try to talk them through it, since they had not really seen stilt walking, firsthand.

I got the stilts in place and proceeded to step up on them and start walking. I was doing quite well, and thinking of my younger days as I started across the lawn, when… one of my stilts went into a small hole in the lawn. The stilts remained in place; I became airborne… forward, over, and down, landing flat on my face. My nose got a bit scraped, which didn't bother me much, but my glasses were a twisted mess! Of course, the grandchild to whom I was demonstrating wasn't sure how he was supposed to react. He was around 12 or 13 at the time. He had believed all his life that Lil' Nana could do anything, but I guess he didn't know that that might include flying and crash-landing.

I think the worst part of that experience was going into the optometrist to get my glasses repaired. "These really got mangled," the girl said to me, taking my glasses. "What happened to them?"

I looked at her, embarrassed, and said, "Well, I was walking on stilts and…"

"Stilts!" she exclaimed as she looked disbelievingly at me. I am sure she was thinking, "This one is definitely a candidate for the funny farm."

There were a few other things besides stilt-walking that had an unwritten rule that "you had to be big enough to pass the test" before you were allowed to do them. For example, you were not allowed to swim in the canal before you could swim well in the pond. The water in the canal was probably about six feet deep, maybe less. I have always been short, so I know it was over my head. The rule in this case certainly made sense, but it also provided a great incentive for the Harbor kids to learn to swim early.

The canal was a cement-enclosed area that was dammed up. Every so often, they would open the dam and drain it, but for the most part, fresh water from the pond constantly ran in and out. Except for heavy drought times, the water was clean and fresh. When you learned to swim well enough to satisfy the older kids, one or more of them would take you to the canal. There, you would "try out." If you could swim across the canal and back in water over your head, you were "in." Most kids were able to do this by the time they were six or seven years old, and the older ones, pretty much, looked after the younger ones. You seldom saw a parent at the canal.

In my years of growing up, I don't remember anyone ever drowning in the canal or in the Harbor pond. I don't even remember any stories about anyone's drowning there. I do know, though, that I almost drowned in the Harbor pond, the summer before I started school. I was just six years old.

I had turned six in May of 1939. That was the summer I learned to do the "dog paddle," but I was not yet a candidate for the canal. Far from it, I found, although I had thought I was pretty good at dog paddling. The problem was that I had only done the dog paddle in the pond and never in water over my head, so the bottom was always within touching distance if reassurance was necessary, or if I got tired.

It was late in August or very early in September and an unusually hot day. There was, for some reason, no older brothers or sisters available to take me swimming, and I remember I started pleading with my mom to take me. I was due to start school in just a few days, and I think that maybe she felt I should be able to go swimming one last time before I was in school all day. It was unusual for my mother to take anyone swimming, because she had never learned to swim, and was quite afraid of the water. In spite of this, she finally agreed to take me for one quick swim.

We arrived at the pond, and there was no one else around. We had the place to ourselves. I proceeded to show her how well I could swim, and she was duly impressed, but warned me not to go out over my head. At the Harbor pond, there was quite a ways that you could walk out and then, suddenly, it dropped off and became quite deep. We called this "the shelf" or "the drop-off." Of course, I had to show her how far out I could go, and proceeded to wade out, calling to her, "See, I can go to here and touch." I went a few steps farther and abruptly the ground seemed to drop out from under me. I immediately forgot everything I had learned about swimming and became panicky, splashing and floundering. My mom jumped up from her spot on the grass and began to wade in, clothes, shoes and all, trying desperately to reach me and calling me to swim to her hand. She was afraid to go out too far, not knowing exactly where the drop-off was, and knowing that if she stepped off it, we would both surely drown.

The last thing I remember was my mother's reaching for me and telling me to swim toward her, but apparently, she realized that she was not going to be able to reach me. To this day, I don't know how she found the courage to do what she did, but when she did realize that she could not reach me, she left me, and went running down the track to the nearest building for help, screaming all the while that I was drowning! I have no memory of her leaving me.

I was told that a young man from town, called "Bun" Liddell, had come running out of the cooperage and sped past my mother to the pond where, I am sure, I had gone down for at least the fated "third time". He had dived in, grabbed me, pulled me out, and laid me face down on the grass. He proceeded to pump water from my lungs with a procedure we used to call "artificial respiration." The next thing I remember was spewing up water.

My mother brought me home and tucked me in bed. It was an experience for me, but I am sure it was much worse for her. I must give her credit, though, because the next day she sent me swimming with one of the older siblings. She was determined I had to go back, so that I wouldn't be afraid of water, as she was. I thank her for that, among many other things. That took a lot of courage, and Maggie had a lot of courage. Unfortunately, I didn't realize what a strong and courageous woman hid behind that quiet, calm exterior until I was much, much older, and a mother myself.

WINTER IN THE HARBOR

Joanne and I had some good times together. We also had our share of squabbles. When we were young, we spent much time together and were constantly in competition for her mother's attention or a pat on the head by my father.

Most of our time was spent just playing, and since we didn't have many toys, most of our play depended on our imaginations and makeshift toys. I think that was a good thing. I don't remember being bored or complaining of having "nothing to do." Besides that, if we did complain, my mother never had a problem finding something for us to do that wasn't play.

In the winter, some of our days were spent playing "dress-up" with old clothes, if we had to be inside, or sliding down the hill next to our house, if the weather permitted. We usually had a sled or two, but if we didn't, a big piece of cardboard or a wooden box could suffice to get us where we wanted to go… to the bottom of the hill. One sister related to me the memory of our father making sleds out of barrel staves. I don't remember that but I am sure it is very possible. At times, if the snow was soft and not crusty, we would spend as much time pushing each other down the hill as we spent pulling our sliding apparatus up the hill.

I loved the snow and cold then, as I do now, (except for the heating bills) but as a child I had a very weak bladder, and more than once, we would get all bundled up in our snow suits, boots, scarf, hats, and mittens, and I would be about a third of the way up the hill when I would begin to feel pressure on my bladder. I knew that I was no good at "holding it" and that I didn't have much time to get inside to the toilet. In spite of this knowledge (which came from many repeated experiences), I would not turn around at that point and start back to the house to pee before I went sliding. It was just so much trouble to get out of all those clothes just to go the toilet!

I always felt sure that this time I could hold it until I got to the top of the hill and slide down at least once. The Patron Saint of Bodily Functions was seldom on my side. I would just about reach the top of the hill and be ready to push off when, no matter what I did, from crossing my legs to holding my snowsuit pants tightly into my crotch (hoping it would act as a temporary plug), the warm urine would begin to flow. By the time I got to the bottom of the hill, I would be wearing a snowsuit that was soggy with what began as warm urine, but had, during the descent, become icy cold against my bottom and my legs.

And so, I would slide to the bottom, get off my sled and go into the house and strip down. My sliding would have ended for that day (or at least for a few hours until my snowsuit was washed and dried (which was no quick or easy task in the winter). Since there were no electric dryers at that time, it was necessary to hang it by the stove in the kitchen or the front room and wait until it dried.

We also liked to ski in the winter. When I see kids now with hundreds of dollars worth of ski equipment, from designer goggles to heavy-duty boots, I am sometimes reminded of our "ski equipment." Our "equipment" consisted of our regular winter clothes and boots and two barrel staves strapped onto our boots with old belts or strips of leather scraps from the leatherboard mill. For poles, we found that two old sticks did just fine.

Now, barrel staves are pretty much a thing of the past, so I will describe them as best I can. In those days, a lot of things came in wooden barrels. The barrels were made of many wide strips of wood that were bent slightly, and then stood on end, side by side to form a circle. Rather like standing popsicle sticks on end, side by side to make a plant holder or something. These long sticks ("staves," as they were called) were then held together by three metal strips that were tightly wrapped around them near the top, middle and bottom. The bottom was made from a disk of wood and attached to one end of the staves, and then a lid was made in the same manner as the bottom.

When these barrels were taken apart, the staves could be used to strap to your feet. As they were curved, slightly bent at the front and back ends, they worked quite nicely as skis for us. The best part is that they were plentiful and free.

Imagination is a wonderful thing. I think, that at that time, I had never seen a real pair of skis. Perhaps I had seen pictures of them, but in my mind, I was soaring down beautiful high slopes, gracefully swerving and swaying. And this was all being done on a pair of barrel staves, using two sticks for ski poles.

I may be wrong, but I seriously doubt that children who have thousand-dollar ski paraphernalia have as wonderful a time as we did with our imagination and those barrel staves strapped on our feet.

Two of my grandsons, Lowell and Chris, were visiting us in Vermont.

My husband (Fred) and I did a fair amount of cross-country skiing and the boys really wanted to ski badly. Not having any barrel staves, of course, I decided that they could have some fun in the field next to our house using <u>our</u> cross-country skis.

It was a sight to see, but they had so much fun. These two little boys, probably around seven or eight years old, were going to learn on skis that were much, much bigger than they were. But, they were game, and so was I. I helped them get into the ski boots, which were much too big for them, strapped the boots onto the skis, gave them the poles and off they went… sort of. They fell. Fred and I helped them to get back into an upright position, they would go forward a few feet, and they would be down again. We all laughed a lot! They gave it a try (and were eager to go out the next day to try again). Best of all, we had created a memory. They both still remember that day and we have laughed about it since, even though they are both now in their twenties.

Of course, we also had the harbor pond at our disposal for winter sports… skating, ice-fishing. No skates? Just bring your sled. If you pick it up and run fast and then plop down on your belly, you can slide a long way on the ice.

Crack the whip was a good skating game as long as you were not the one on the end of the whip. Did you ever play crack the whip? You need as many kids as you can get… all sizes, all on skates. They will line up holding hands and start skating very fast. It works best if a big strong boy is at the head of the line. Everybody starts skating, faster, faster, and then, when you are at about top speed, the first guy (the strong boy) stops abruptly and s-w-i-i-n-g-s the whole whip in an arc behind him. A chain reaction! It really is fun. Well, maybe not quite as fun for the little guy/girl at the end because they will either fall down and slide across the ice, or let go and go sailing, faster than the speed of light, it seems, all alone across the pond.

When it started getting dark, or even after dark, a bunch of old tires would be retrieved from various barns and fields and brought to the pond. They would be stacked fairly high and then someone would pour a little kerosene on them, throw a lighted match into the pile, and we would have an amazing, smoking, high, bright, bon fire.

It would smell bad. Old tires smell awful when they burn, and the smoke!!! Talk about pollution! We could have sent smoke signals to the Indians in Arizona if we could have gotten close enough to that bon fire to throw a wet blanket over it. The smoke was thick, black and nasty, but oh did it throw some great warm waves of heat to keep us thawed out.

We stayed away from the center of the pond until deep winter because we were told there was a "channel" that ran through the center and since it was rapidly moving water, it took much longer for the ice to freeze in that spot. Sometimes, while skating, we would hear a loud rumbling-like c-r-a-c-k, and could at times feel the ice reverberate under our feet. They used to say that was the ice settling. I'm not sure, but it didn't feel very safe to me.

As winter began warming into spring, the "brick steamer" would reappear in our minds and young lovers would come, hand in hand and sit "spooning" while the native Harborite would try to convince a new boyfriend/girlfriend that the brick steamer really did exist. The brick steamer story lasted for decades and during that time, many a young couple sat watching for it. I wonder if that story is still used? If not, all you young Townsend Harborites are missing out on a good thing! But I haven't yet told you about the brick steamer.

The brick steamer was an important part of some of the folklore that existed in Townsend Harbor. The brick steamer was not a boat that carried bricks into the harbor, but was, in the folklore, a steamboat made of bricks! Native boys or girls, when dating, would take their date up to the Harbor pond and sit on the bank, trying to convince their date that there was indeed, a brick steamer that would be coming around the point that jutted out into the water, any time now. Of course, you had to do something while you were waiting for the steamer to appear, so a bit of hugging and kissing helped pass the time. Unless you were dating a total moron, your date quickly figured out the game but they went along with it… for obvious reasons.

My husband proposed to me on the banks of the Harbor Pond while we were laughingly waiting for the brick steamer, (for probably about the fortieth time). At that point, we had been dating since we were both in high school, and so we were well past the stage where I even pretended to try to fool him. It remains, though, a really nice memory that I treasure.

Sadly, "courting," or just plain dating, isn't like that anymore. I'm not sure if we have gained or lost a treasured and gentle tradition that also had its humorous side. I haven't lost it. It is forever locked in my memory bank. A simpler time, a simpler place, a contented couple whose marriage lasted for forty-six years, until death parted us.

SEX ED... LEARNED, NOT TAUGHT

Have any of you ever wondered if there was sex education in the 1930s and 1940s? If you have, wonder no more, because I have a couple of stories to tell you that will explain a little about how, as children, we obtained our sex education. That is, of course, if you lived in a farm community in a small town in Massachusetts. I have no idea what the rest of the world was doing with it at that time.

Yes! There was sex education, but I, and most of us at a young age, didn't know that it was either sex or educational. We didn't know about the "birds and the bees," but we did know about the "cats and the cows." Living on a small family farm, and having a large farm just up the road, provided us with many opportunities to learn.

Unlike many, or perhaps most kids who were growing up at that time, we sometimes observed a bull mounting a cow. Of course, this only happened occasionally because most adults were not into calling out to kids to see the animals mate. But it was difficult, I imagine, to send us away during the heat of bovine passion, or need, or instinct, or whatever it is with bovines.

The first time I saw it happen, when I was about eight years old, I thought the cow was trying to give the bull a piggyback, and I thought it was quite exciting. I had no idea at that time what the likely outcome of that piggyback would be, but it was one of the first pieces of a puzzle that, eventually, became the whole sex picture.

I, of course, had seen chickens lay their eggs and was puzzled when one of them would choose to set on the eggs and keep them warm until they hatched. The "broody hen" would peck at you if you tried to take those eggs out from under her and bring them in to cook for breakfast.

My mother had told me not to reach under a particular hen because she wanted her to produce chicks from this setting. It was too tempting. I went out to collect the eggs and there sat Miss Mollie, quietly clucking and watching me with her black beady eyes. When chickens are nesting, their clucking is a low, soft, contented "cluck" sound, almost musical, as though hushing potential chicks with her calmness. I sneaked around and up behind her, reached under her into the soft warm hay that was her nest, and my hand felt either three or four eggs.

As her contented "cluck, cluck," turned into an angry squawk, I grabbed a big brown egg. I put it into the basket with the others I had collected and ran for the kitchen. Fresh eggs for breakfast!

Mom took the eggs from me and washed them in the sink . Then she chose three to crack open into a sizzling pan of bacon grease. The first one was sputtering and crackling beautifully, browning up around the edges, when she tried to crack open the second. It cracked and she dumped into the fry pan a scrawny, naked, half-formed chick with a whole lot of slimy goop around it. I instantly knew that was the one I had stolen from the broody hen. I cried… hard! Mom took the spatula, lifted the tiny, naked, gray-colored corpse out of the pan and tossed it in the garbage.

"I'm sorry, I'm sorry, Mama." She knew instantly what had happened.

"Don't go near the setting hens again. You wouldn't like it if someone stole you from your mama."

She left it at that, and so did I, but I did wonder... How come there was a chicken in that egg? And how come it was so weird looking? And why wasn't a chick in any other egg? I was not yet bright enough to start putting it all together. It was a long time before I realized that the hens only had eggs that were fertile (could grow into baby chicks) when the rooster was hanging around. Another piece of the puzzle fell into place.

A still later experience gave me a bit more in my "Introduction to Sex Education" life courses. A family who used to live in the old schoolhouse up on the back road hill, moved next door to us. There was a large field between our houses, but it was "next door" to us. This family had several children, maybe five. Among the children were two older boys, perhaps 12 and 14, and a girl, Glenda, who was about a year or so younger than I. Glenda was my first real playmate that wasn't related to me, and I know I was happy to have her move nearby. I suspect she felt the same since she, like me, had two brothers next in age to her and also like me, had no close-in-age sisters.

When I was around 10 years old, two of the boys, (whether they were her brothers, my brothers or one of each, I'm not sure) approached us excitedly while we were playing in the field.

"There's a safe hanging on the fence up the back road!" They sounded excited. "You oughta go see it! It's hanging right on the barb wire fence by the old school driveway!"

Glenda and I dropped whatever we were doing and immediately hightailed across the field, through the woods on the path that was a shortcut to the old school... all the way talking about this amazing phenomena that the boys had seen! A safe! Hanging on a fence! We could not imagine how it had gotten there or how it could be hanging on a fence!

Coming out of the woods and crossing the old back road, we saw the fence they were talking about, but no matter how hard we looked (and we knew a safe hanging there would be pretty big and pretty obvious), we couldn't see it. Figuring the boys had "got us" again, we trekked home, down the hill to the harbor. No shortcut this time. We needed the extra time to talk about this and probably we were figuring out a plan to get back at them for fooling us.

I know that I told Charlotte about it. I don't know if I told her immediately or shortly after, but I did say to her, "The boys fooled us. They told us there was a safe hanging on the fence up by the old school driveway, and Glenda and I walked all the way up there, and there wasn't any safe! All we found hanging on that old barb wire fence was a little white balloon, and it was broken." Charlotte immediately burst out laughing. She didn't explain to me what the balloon/safe was, probably figuring I was much too young, but she occasionally brings that story up and kids me about finding a "safe hanging on the fence." It was quite a few years after that before I found out that a "safe" was another word for condom, or "rubbers" as they were sometimes called. And so, I put that piece of the puzzle in its place. It was starting to come together. The outside framework was nearly finished, and I was just <u>starting</u> to figure out what, <u>maybe</u>, the whole picture might be.

I think I was eleven when I was spending a couple of weeks in the summer at my sister Margaret's house in Providence, R.I. Joey and I were taking my nephew, Milton, to the park that day. Roger Williams Park was one of our favorite places to go. They had a sort of playground, and after you crossed the parking lot, then crossed the playground/picnic area, there was a small amusement park, complete with merry-go-round and a calliope playing. We loved that merry-go-round!

One day we took the trolley car to the park and got off, as we always did, at the entrance to the parking lot. Clutching our lunch bags in one hand and our precious nickels in the other (and still managing to hang on to my nephew, Milton), we started across the parking lot, heading for the picnic area. We always wanted to get lunch out of the way first, thus giving us the whole afternoon of uninterrupted playtime.

While crossing the parking lot, Joey said, "Look at that guy over there, Ally. What's he doing?"

I looked across the way and there was a man, sitting in the front seat of his car... door open, one foot in the car, the other out on the ground, zipper on his pants down with the fly wide open, masturbating. At that time I had no idea about masturbation. Some little voice inside was telling me that he was doing something wrong... mostly because everyone knew it wasn't nice to open up your pants and "show yourself" out in public. I didn't know he was masturbating. That word or the concept was not yet familiar to me.

"What's he doing?" Joey repeated.

Of course, I had been the older (by 22 months) and wiser since we were very small, and I was not about to let her think I didn't have an answer for her now! "He's just exercising it," I told her, matter of factly, "and we shouldn't be watching! It's private." And with that, we grabbed Milton's hand and made our way to enjoy the rest of the day.

Somewhere, somehow, I think we both knew what we saw was wrong because neither of us mentioned it to Margaret. I don't remember discussing the incident further with Joey, but I think we were both fairly certain that if we did tell Margaret, that would have ended our weekly sojourns to the park... and that was the last thing we wanted to happen!

There are few puzzle pieces with formal sex education. The puzzle is presented in its entirety in just a few quick classes... not dragged out, piece by tantalizing piece over the years. I know that for a fact because I taught sex ed for several years. One of the problems, as I see it, is that it is rather like giving a youngster who just got his license, a new car. He has the car, but it came so fast and so easy to him that it has less value than if he had had to build it, or work for it. We give kids all the information, but we cannot give them the wherewithal to value, cherish, and use it selectively and gently. That is probably a poor analogy but it's the best I can do for now. Otherwise, I'll start preaching, and neither the writer nor the reader wants that.

ALLY'S MUSICAL DEBUT

New clothes were not something we received often, but thanks to a man by the name of "Mr. Miller," we did get new clothes for special occasions. One Memorial Day was just such an occasion for me.

A gentleman with a big gray car used to stop at our house weekly. He was a rather short, stout man who always seemed to be dressed in nice clothes… usually a suit. I remember him only as "Mr. Miller," and my memory tells me he came on Monday, but that may not be accurate. This man was a door-to-door peddler and brought with him large assortments of clothes, and perhaps other items that were not important to me, so I didn't notice. I was only interested in the little girls' clothes.

Mr. Miller was a nice, pleasant man and he allowed his customers to pay him small amounts each week on their purchases. At least I know he did that with my mother… an early version of the credit card system, except that it was door-to-door delivery and collection.

I recall one year when I was in fourth grade, I was given a large part in the school's Memorial Day play. The part included a long song ("America The Beautiful") that I was to sing, solo. Two or three verses! I was thrilled, and told my mother I would need a white dress for that solo. When Mr. Miller came, my mom told him what was needed. The following week, he came back with two different white dresses in my size. They were both very beautiful to me. My mother picked the one with a full skirt and a wide white satin or taffeta sash around the waist. I suspect the least expensive. It had pouffy short sleeves, and around the neck was a wide ruffle that extended out to the shoulders. (When I think back on it now, it was rather like a clown's collar.) It was frilly, and to me, it was beautiful. I loved it. The best part was that I got white Mary Jane shoes to go with it.

The Memorial Day pageant day arrived and a large group of students were on stage. The moment came when I, resplendent in my white dress and shiny white patent leather shoes, stepped forward. The piano introduction played and I, at the top of my lungs, belted out "America The Beautiful." It was my moment. No opera star ever presented a song as proudly or feelingly as I did that day. The applause from the audience was great. I bowed and became a bit teary-eyed… whether with nerves or just plain awe, I'm not sure. For a little blond girl from "The Harbor" in her new white dress with the big ruffled collar and new Mary Jane shoes, it was a magical moment.

FOOD FOR THE TAKING?

There were lots of things that we didn't have as we were growing up, but there were also a lot of things that we did have. For treats, we had fresh-canned peaches or pears that tasted almost like they had just been picked from the tree. We had homemade canned blueberries, that when brought up from the cellar and turned over to my mom, would magically be turned into a delicious blueberry pie. Apple turnovers were another favorite. And fresh mince pie! I could go on and on and on. We had fresh, whole milk, straight from the cow, and eggs fresh from the chickens. There was not, that I can remember, any lack of food in our house.

There were a lot of different kinds of deliverymen at that time. For example, there was the oilman, the iceman, the ragman, the bread man, and the milkman, to name a few. We didn't usually use the bread man or the milkman because, as I have said, we had a cow to supply us with milk, and my mother baked our bread… that I didn't really like. I loved store bread. Well, actually I liked homemade bread when it was warm and fresh from the oven. I even liked it when it was a few hours old (especially the crusty ends), but because it had no preservatives, it didn't stay as soft and as fresh as I liked it. And we seldom got "store" bread. I would, at times, trade my sandwich at lunchtime in school because other kids liked homemade bread. I could get a tuna salad sandwich in trade for a peanut butter sandwich on homemade bread. I didn't care about the filling…I just cared that their sandwiches were made with soft spongy store bread!

I don't know how old I was, maybe around seven, but I was walking down Main Street one day and, on a neighbor's porch, I saw a fresh loaf of bread that had been delivered to her by the bread man. She lived several houses up the street from us, and apparently she was not home when he came, so he had just left it for her. This was a fairly common practice if you had routine deliveries. It was so tempting! I carefully looked around and saw no one, so I quickly walked up to the porch and carefully unsealed one end of the bread wrapper (no twisty ties in those days), removed the end piece and took the next two pieces out. Replacing the end piece, I folded over the opened wrapper and placed that end against the door, thinking that Mrs. G. wouldn't notice, or maybe think the glue that was holding it together had come unstuck. Little did I know that the lady who lived across the street had been watching me. She didn't call out to me or anything, but it wasn't too long before my mother got the news that I had been seen "stealing" bread. My mother was mortified! All the bread I could eat at our house, and I was taking someone else's! Believe me, I did get a talking to that day. She might not have been as embarrassed if it had even been a candy bar or something we seldom had… but bread! That was something that some people in town even paid her to make for them occasionally. But nobody understood that it wasn't just any old bread… it was soft, spongy store bread that brought out the devil in me!

When my mother was making fresh churned butter, I would wait for her to finish so I could lick the butter bowl. While most kids loved licking the cake batter or frosting from the stirring spoon or the mixing bowl, my favorite was the butter bowl. When the milk was brought in from the cow, it was left to set on the counter in the pantry for a while. This allowed the cream in the milk to rise to the top. When the cream had formed a nice, sometimes quite thick, pale yellowish cover over the top of the milk, my mother would skim the cream off and it would be churned, with a little salt added, into butter. I don't remember my mother ever making whipped cream. I imagine that all the cream was turned into butter.

The making of butter was another cooking lesson that was (accidentally) passed on not too long ago. My oldest grandson, Eric was in my kitchen cooking with me. He was making whipped cream with my new, heavy-duty electric beater. I looked over at him and said, casually, "Watch that, Eric! That beater is powerful and you might end up with butter if you're not careful." He looked at me and said "Really? This could really turn into butter?" I explained to him how you made butter with whipping cream and a little salt (no sugar) and he was truly amazed. Only a week or so later he called to tell me how he had impressed his girlfriend. They were making dinner together and he, nonchalantly, announced that he was going to make fresh butter to put on their garlic bread… and make it he did! She was duly impressed, and I'm sure he made points in that relationship. But once again, I have digressed.

Every once in a while (and it didn't happen too often), we would all be up in bed, sometimes asleep, when we would hear my father's voice call up the stairs, "If anyone wants ice cream, they'd better get down here!" ICE CREAM! You have to understand that ice cream was not something that we got very often. In fact, it was something that we very seldom got. First of all, we had no freezer to store it, and secondly, it was not a necessity. As I have said, we had plenty of pies and homemade pastries, canned fruits, vegetables, meat, and homemade bread… but not ice cream. When we heard that call, we would jump out of bed and hightail it down the stairs where we would find a very small dish of ice cream served up for each of us. It seems that the amount that Pop brought home was probably a quart – maybe even just a pint. I'm not sure because we did, indeed, each get a very small serving… but I remember being so happy and fortunate to get that. I don't recall anyone complaining about the size of the serving, and I sincerely doubt we ever thought about asking for more. Somehow, we knew we were lucky to get any at all.

Yes, that stern, intimidating man who was raising a passel of kids on something like $7.00 a week would take a portion of that hard-earned money and buy ice cream for us. That was another peek at his sensitive side. After we ate the ice cream, he would say in his usual stern, abrupt tone, "Alright now, get back to bed and get to sleep." And so we would go, with the taste of that wonderful cold sweetness still on our lips and in our mouths. He really did love his kids, but could never say it. Instead, he bought an occasional container of ice cream to say it for him.

DASTARDLY DEEDS

Halloween was a great time for us, as it was and still is for kids all over. One difference, however, may have been the freedom we were allowed in roaming all over the little village of Townsend Harbor, where everyone knew everyone else. Our parents felt that we were safe, even if it got to be 9 or 10 o'clock at night. As we got older we expanded our territory to Townsend Center, which was two miles away. There was no "trick or treat" for us, maybe because most households in the 1930s and 1940s had all they could do to feed their own families, much less buy candy for a bunch of the neighborhood kids.

I had never heard of "trick or treat" at that time. Halloween was simply a time to dress up, probably more to disguise us so the neighbors wouldn't know who was doing the tricks (and thus be unable to report to our parents), than for any other reason. When I think back, though, we had no real costumes and no real masks, but would sometimes decorate a paper bag and put it over our heads.

No doubt if they looked closely, they would have recognized my father's old pants or jacket or my mother's old dress.

I remember one Halloween when it was cold and I sneaked my mother's old wool robe from her bedroom and went down the back stairs to the shed. There, I put it on over my heavy jacket, and tied it in the middle with a rope to pull it up so I wouldn't trip on it. I added one of her old "dress" hats from the big box and set out, thinking I was in complete disguise. In fact, if the neighbors didn't recognize the robe, they probably did recognize the hat, and since I was the littlest of the Conner kids, it would not have been too difficult to identify me.

At that point in my life, the most exciting and "bad" trick I had played was to stick a pin in someone's doorbell so that it would keep ringing until they came out. We would stand around the corner of the house, and get a big charge out of it when the person would come out and make a big show of looking all around (as though trying to see who was ringing the doorbell), before removing the pin. I imagine most people with doorbells had been dealing with this trick for many Halloweens, but they never let us down. They always went through the head-scratching, puzzled look routine before removing the pin.

One year, when we were a bit older, we decided to get revenge on a grouchy old man in town who would never let us play near his yard. Mr. L. would yell at us if we were anywhere near his house. He lived in the first house over the bridge in the Harbor, and the dam was kitty-cornered across the road from his house. This particular night several of the Harbor kids, probably between the ages of 10 and 14, or thereabouts, collected eggs (for a week or more) as well as a few old feather pillows. On Halloween night we proceeded not only to pelt his house with eggs, but also to cut open the pillows and empty them on his lawn. It was a very foggy, damp night and the feathers made a soggy mess. After completing this "dastardly deed," we climbed down and scampered in behind the waterfall where we hid, for what seemed like hours, but was probably only 10 or 15 minutes, before the police came and shined their light on the waterfall. They knew where we were hiding, but we stood our ground and would not come out. There was little or no chance that the police chief was going to climb down and come after us.

In our small town, as I have said, everyone knew everyone else, and the police chief was no exception. It did not take a Barney Fife to figure out who the culprits were most likely to be. After giving a few scary sweeps of his spotlight on the waterfall, the police chief went on his merry way. We, feeling very wicked and quite smug, sneaked from behind the falls, climbed up the rocks and scampered home… sure that we had gotten away with one of the most evil crimes ever enacted in Townsend Harbor.

Our little fantasy lasted until the next morning when, bright and early, "Uncle Bud" (as the police chief was called by the kids in town), appeared at the doorsteps of the wanted criminals, and we were instructed to bring buckets of water and rakes to Mr. L.'s house. There, we spent most of the morning scrubbing what we could reach on the house and raking up wet feathers. Mr. L. never showed his grouchy face while we were there, but after we finished, "Uncle Bud" gave us each a nickel and a scolding that deterred us from trying to get even with Mr. L. again. This was long before Community Service was ever heard of!

PEARL HARBOR DAY

December 7, 1941, was a remarkable day in history, but as an eight-year-old child, I had no idea of the enormity of the act or even where or what Pearl Harbor was.

I remember several people sitting around our kitchen table that Sunday morning, when a friend of my father came in the back door and said, "Did you hear… the Japs just bombed Pearl Harbor?" My father jumped up from the table and ran through the door leading to the shed and called up the back stairs to my brother Larry. Larry, age 19, was home on leave from the Navy. He came running down the back stairs and into the kitchen, very angry and upset. I don't remember what he said, but I do remember thinking that he was mad because his leave would be cut short. I also remember feeling sad because my brother would be leaving again long before his "vacation" was over.

I think children were much more sheltered from the bad news in the world at that time. We had no televisions blaring out at us, only the radio, which was not, that I can remember, ever on during the day, but only turned on when my father listened to the news in the evening. It was usually left on after that for the evening programs. My brother Larry was immediately called back to duty, and so the war entered into my little world.

The war was exciting for us. It didn't seem, at my age, that it was real. I saw no graphic pictures of bombings and bodies and wounded servicemen, and heard very little that affected me. In fact, it provided what we kids saw as local excitement. We would, fairly frequently, hear a rumbling sound in the distance, and would run out to the front of the house to watch the army tanks and trucks moving slowly up Rt. 119, our Main Street, past our house on their way to… we knew not where. The trucks were usually carrying supplies, artillery, and uniformed men who would wave at us as they went by. The lumbering tanks were very big and very noisy and most of all, very impressive to the kids standing only about 30 feet away from them, watching and waving.

There was a large field between our house and the next house up the street. This field was used for a lot of things from drying the sheets of leatherboard from the factory across the street, to serving as a ball field for kids in the summer. It was a much more exciting field during the war years when, occasionally, planes used it for target practice. The planes would fly over, dip down, and drop bags of flour in the field. My mother would sternly caution us to stay in the house until the "bombing" was over.

At night we had to be sure all the shades, called "blackout shades," were pulled down over the windows so there would be no light shining through. That part was rather scary to me. I believed that if a light did shine out from our house, we would be seen from the air, and the enemy would bomb our house. I knew the war was far away, but wasn't too sure that it couldn't sneak in on us at night if our lights were on.

In the pre-war days, at school we used to have fire drills, but now we had air raid drills. The fire drills were more fun because we got to line up when the bell clanged and march outside and get a break from the classroom. During the air raid drills, when the bell rang, we would be instructed to get under our desks instead of going outside. I always wondered if that desk was going to protect me if a bomb hit us;

somehow, I never was brave enough to ask.

Letters would come from my brother, but they were not the usual type of letter. It was called "V Mail" and was like a letter that had been shrunk. On these letters, sometimes, single words or whole sentences were blacked out. This censoring prevented the troops from inadvertently giving out information that might be crucial to the war effort. They would not, in most cases, be allowed to write home and tell where they would be transferred to, for example.

In the front window of our house hung a small flag, maybe measuring 10" x 12". This flag had a white background and a single star that took up a good portion of the center of the flag. Homes that had family members serving in the armed forces would have this type of flag hanging in the window. If you had two or three family members serving, there would be that same number of stars on the flag, to let the world know how proud you were of them.

On the day the Japanese surrendered, a lot of neighborhood kids were swimming in the canal. It was a hot August day, and we were horsing around as usual, when the sirens began sounding. Church bells were ringing, the mill whistle was blowing… anything that could make noise in the village was making noise. We knew instantly what was happening, and we started yelling and screaming, "The war is over, the war is over!" and jumping into the water for a victory swim. It was a grand and exciting day, even for a bunch of young kids.

OUR VOLUNTEER FIRE DEPARTMENT

In the shed, hung a large burlap sack we called "the can bag." It hung on a nail just outside the kitchen door, and whenever a can was emptied (and since my mother home-canned most of our food herself in glass jars, there weren't many real cans), the can was thrown into the can bag. The can bag would not have been any big deal except for the fact that my father always kept his rubber boots on the floor, just under the can bag. If they hadn't been kept there, I would have no story. These rubber boots were special in that they were his "fireman's boots," and were a much heavier rubber boot than normal. They were not big, high boots, but came to just below the knees.

The can bag also held bottle caps and anything else that was metal. We would open the back kitchen door and toss the can or bottle cap or can lid out, and (hopefully) it would end in the can bag. Our aim was not always accurate, however, and at times a bottle cap or two would land in Mickey's boot(s).

A few days, or even a few weeks, would pass and then, all at once, perhaps in the middle of the night, the fire siren would go off. My father would jump out of bed and pull on his clothes, run down the back stairs, and on his way to the kitchen door, grab his boots. Once inside the kitchen, he would quickly jam his feet into his boots. As soon as this happened, the fact was known throughout the house (if not throughout the neighborhood) that at least one or more bottle caps had missed the can bag... and landed in Mickey's boot! Mickey would be yelling and hopping around, trying to get the boot back off in a hurry to relieve his injured foot, dump out the bottle caps, put the boot back on, and go out the door to run to the firehouse (which was at the corner, about a short block away). This ritual was almost as predictable as the aforementioned morning ritual for going to work. I must say, however, it was considerably noisier.

As I have said before, Townsend Harbor was a very small town, and everyone knew everyone else. I hear people say that about small towns now, but I <u>really</u> mean that everyone really <u>did</u> know everyone else. There were not a lot of things that happened in our little town that were exciting, and so when the fire alarm went off, not just the firemen (who were unpaid volunteers), would jump up. Just about everyone in town would jump up, and usually before the fire was anywhere near under control, people would begin arriving. If it were at night, people would be in their nightclothes, standing around watching a neighbor's barn or house burn, and providing whatever support they could. I believe it was not because they were nosy, but more because they were concerned.

If it were a brush fire that could last a while, the women would sometimes go home and make sandwiches and coffee and bring them to the men who were fighting the fire. It probably sounds rather callous that we all... men, women, and children were chasers of the fire truck. In reality, it was a rather nice thing. Not, of course that neighbors were losing their property, but because of the closeness, the caring, and the sharing of bad times. It was a feeling that is hard to describe clearly to anyone who has not experienced it.

I guess, when I really think about it, the fire department in a small town at that time was a pretty special thing. We didn't have much for entertainment. Oh, we had the minstrel shows, but I am not sure that they weren't put on by the fire department… and they only happened once or twice a year. We had clambakes every summer, and they were put on by the fire department also.

The firehouse was heated all winter in order that the trucks could be kept warm and ready for emergency calls. Next to the bay where the trucks were kept, was a small room that had a couple of chairs and a television set. I think the fire department had a TV before we had one in our house, and brother Larry would sometimes (along with some other men in the neighborhood, I'm sure), go up to the firehouse and watch television in the evening. If it happened to be a frigid night in winter, there were times when he, rather than trek home in the cold, would climb onto the front seat of one of the fire trucks (we had two) and sleep for the night.

Yes… a siren, two fire trucks, limited equipment, and a bunch of rag-tag men, possibly risking their lives, but dedicated to saving the property, animals, or lives of their neighbors. A large part of the backbone of our community.

That was our Volunteer Fire Department.

CLAMBAKES

The clambakes were really big events. We would look forward to that outing as soon as the summer started. Everybody in town, from the oldest to the youngest, would attend this annual shindig.

The firemen would have huge tubs set over an open fire where they would steam the clams. Another tub would have corn-on-the-cob cooking. When the food was done, people would line up and receive a plate full of steaming little-neck clams and a big, fresh ear of corn- on-the-cob, and a little dish of sweet butter to dip the clams in. I can still taste them, and whenever I see them fresh in the market (for a reasonable price), I buy some and bring them home and steam them. They still taste good, but somehow, never as good as at the clambakes.

After everyone had their bellies full, the firemen would have "entertainment" for us. This entertainment consisted of a "Firemen's Muster," usually a race between the fire departments of Townsend Harbor, Townsend Center, and West Townsend. The race was to see who could get out of their beds, get into their clothes, and man the hoses the quickest. They were being timed, which put a bit more pressure on them.

The men who were participating would lie on folding cots that were supposed to represent their beds. They would be dressed only in their long johns or union suits. The alarm would ring, and they had to jump out of bed, get into their pants, shirts, and boots, then run and grab the hoses and pretend to put out a fire. The funny part was that they would be running as they were trying to get dressed, tripping over their pant legs, and trying to get their boots on while running. Of course, as kids, we thought it was hysterical just to see grown men running around outside in their underwear! The crowd would yell and cheer them on. Somehow, it doesn't seem as funny on paper. I guess you had to be there… and I'm glad I was.

Another event was the "greased pig" contest. They would put grease all over a small pig and turn it loose, and people would try to catch it. Anyone who wanted to, joined in. There was a prize for the winner.

I remember one time, I had a white dress on, (maybe my Memorial Day dress) and the pig ran by me, squealing loudly, and my white dress became smeared with black grease. I wasn't even in the contest, because of the white dress (and probably I was too young anyway), but I think I could have caught that pig that day. I am sure that game no longer exists. The SPCA would have a fit and would say we were being cruel to the animal. In a way, I guess it was, but it was fun.

MY FATHER, THE END MAN

My father was a minstrel man. He was also a carpenter, a gardener, a fireman, a bricklayer, a millwright, a trolley car driver, a farmer and a host of other things in his lifetime, but he loved the minstrel and all the old songs and dances that went with it. He was an "end man" in the local minstrel shows in Townsend.

A minstrel show is a thing of the past, of course, since the world has become nearly obsessed with prejudices… and ethnic jokes are no longer allowed. I am not saying that the change is all bad, but I do think it's a shame we can no longer laugh at others or ourselves without being accused of being prejudiced. I think we have all become too sensitive and so thin-skinned that we diligently look for things that we can claim to be offended about.

Minstrel shows were discontinued because it was felt by some that parts of the shows contained racial slurs against black people. The performers in minstrel shows were white men who would blacken their faces and sing and dance and tell jokes. As I see it, these were not necessarily jokes about the black people, but jokes that black people told among themselves, being repeated by white men in black faces. I may be very wrong about that. In looking back, I do know that there were many people who were prejudiced, and I can say that I understand how people might be upset about white men blackening their faces and entertaining audiences with their antics. I am not sure, however, that in some aspects, we have become too much a nation filled with politically correct, ultra-sensitive people, and because of that, we have lost our sense of humor.

At any rate, prejudiced or not, Mickey was a damned fine minstrel man and a great end man. The end men sat on each side of the stage, near the front. There were usually two on each side and between the singing and dancing acts, the end men would make jokes and do some clowning around with each other and the audience. They were generally dressed in wigs and costumes and had their faces blackened, I think with charcoal. Some of those costumes lived in the big box in our house, upstairs under the sloping ceiling.

Some of the Conner kids performed at one time or another in the minstrel shows. I know I was fairly young when Charlotte sang a song in one of the shows. I am not positive, but I think the song might have been "Mexicali Rose." I am sure if I am wrong, she'll correct me on that one.

The minstrel shows were held in the Town Hall in Townsend Center. There were also talent shows held there occasionally. I never had a chance to sing in the minstrel show, but did strut my stuff in one of the talent shows. The song was "Oh Johnny," and I can't remember if someone picked it out for me ,or if I chose it myself. I don't know whether or not prizes were given at the talent shows, but if they were, I know I didn't win one. That, I am sure I would remember if it had happened!

MAGGIE'S LEGACY, HOME COOKIN'

I know that I have used considerable space telling about Maggie, but she is a very large part of who I am, and what in my life contributed to what I am today… my grandchildren's Lil' Nana.

Although I did not acquire Maggie's calm demeanor and lady-like presence, her cooking blood flows strongly in my veins. I agree with scientists that a large part of who we are is genetic, but I also think that learned behavior is sort of the icing on the genetic cake. Since this chapter is about home cooking, I will dip my finger into that icing and try to paint a sweet picture for you.

As I said before, Maggie practically grew up in a bakery. According to her, she and my grandfather would arrive at the bakery very early, maybe 3 or 4 in the morning, and start baking the bread for the early customers. I imagine this was accomplished by making the dough the night before (as she used to do when we were growing up), covering it, and letting it rise until morning, when it would be punched down, set in pans to rise again, and then popped in the oven. When I make bread, I will often do that, too, so that not only is the bread ready to bake in the morning, but also so there is fresh dough ready to make the beloved "dough cakes" for breakfast. I will explain dough cakes a little later.

One day we were in the kitchen and she kneeled down to get something out of the oven or pick something up from the floor, and I heard her knees make a "crack" sound.

I said to her "Mom, how come your knees make that noise?" She told me that one day, when she was young and working in the bakery, an elderly lady came in to buy a loaf of bread. The fresh bread was kept in a glass case that was under the customer counter. She kneeled down to get the bread from the case, and her knees "cracked." Embarrassed, she handed the bread to the lady and said, "I guess I must be getting old."

The lady replied, "No, dear, that doesn't mean you are getting old. That means you will always hold lots of babies on those knees." My knees crack when I kneel down. I have four children, eight grandchildren, and six great- grandchildren. Thankfully, I guess my knees didn't crack as much as Maggie's!

But I am reminiscing and getting off the point, so back to the story.

Growing up in Maggie's kitchen was, in retrospect, a wonderful experience. I learned so many things that I still use today... mainly the love of cooking, and how rewarding it is to see people devour and praise the food you have prepared and put before them. There is such satisfaction in seeing four or five pies lined up on the counter, ready for family, company, or dessert for a Thanksgiving dinner. I nearly always made at least four, and usually five different kinds to be sure I had all the family favorites: apple for Andy, blueberry for Larry, lemon meringue for Skip, chocolate cream for Rick, and pumpkin for my husband, Fred. Even though Fred is no longer with us, on holidays I still make a pumpkin pie for the few pumpkin lovers of the family.

There are still a few women who "can" foods, but I think they are few and far between. I learned this skill by helping my mother in the kitchen, and even though I do not "need" to have jars of food lined up on the shelves in the cellar-way anymore, I somehow feel a compulsion to do at least a few jars when autumn arrives, and the fruits and vegetables are fresh and plentiful.

My favorites (homemade spaghetti sauce, plum, peach and grape preserves, whole tomatoes, and the grandchildren's favorite… dill pickles) are always added to my shelves each canning season. Many, many jars of pickles are made each year! I have made homemade mincemeat too; there is nothing that smells better when bubbling on the stove than mincemeat with its chopped apples, raisins and spices. Green tomato relish is a close second, though.

It pleases me no end that all my grandchildren love to cook. Chris and Lowell prefer to do their cooking on the grill outside, and that is okay with me! I'll man the kitchen while you man the grill…meet you in the dining room!

All of my grandchildren have, at one time or another assisted me in the making of dill pickles. They love doing it and each summer one or more of them will say to me, "Nan, be sure to call me when it's time to make the pickles, so that I can come and help." Lee Anne ("Lanny") is the one granddaughter who has not shared the love for cooking… but, soon to be married, she is learning. She does, however, love to make pickles (even though she doesn't care to eat them). Lanny is in banking and has other valuable talents and skills that I have never possessed… the greatest of these being that she excels in accounting, and managing money. I laughingly tell her that these talents will be very necessary for me in my old age. When all of the others are doing their part to assist me in my infirmities, i.e. changing my diaper, wiping my drool, cooking my food and feeding me, etc., she can be managing my accounts and paying the bills.

Granddaughter, Sadie, has made pickles on her own, in her own kitchen with my recipe. I am reasonably sure many of the others will follow. Not a bad legacy to pass on, I think.

I loved the smell of my mother's kitchen. It seemed that there was almost always something cooking. I was reminded of that not too long ago when Skip, second oldest of my sons, was talking with others about favorite foods they remembered from when they were growing up. He told them, "I loved the food, but most of all, I remember how good it smelled when I came into the kitchen. You always knew what was cooking... brownies, fish chowder, pies, stew... it always smelled good." That was one of the nicest compliments I could have had... it was how I felt about my mother's kitchen.

Andy, my youngest (referred to by all as "the Cookie Monster"), lives about a mile away from me, but I swear he can smell cookies baking from across-town. He will come into the house, and if no cookies are apparent in the glass cookie jar, he will ferret them out, no matter where I might hide them. When he was younger, at times I would wrap them and put them in the freezer, labeled "SQUASH." That was the only way I could save some for the future.

My two other sons, Larry, the oldest, and Rick, our third, have a love for eating but also have the passed-down love for cooking, and both of them have canned their own sauces and made their own preserves and proudly serve them when I visit... and the beat(er) goes on.

My sons grew up cranking the old "food grinder" that I would attach to the shelf. They, and their children after them, loved turning the crank to grind up the tomatoes, peppers, turkey giblets, and anything else that needed grinding, with the same old grinder that was used in my mother's kitchen when I was a child. (I don't think they loved grinding the onions. That is a pretty powerful smell.)

When we were growing up, our fare, while plentiful, was simple. Meat, potatoes, vegetables, and of course, desserts. Breakfast on weekend mornings was one of our favorites. The dough would have risen the night before, and when we got up and came downstairs for breakfast, Mom would have a large fry pan with bacon grease or lard heating on the stove. She would take pieces from the punched down dough, stretch them out into rather long pieces and lay them in the hot bacon grease, or melted lard. They would start bubbling and browning up, and when the color was just right, she would turn them over to brown on the other side. When they were ready, she would remove them and place them on a large platter and repeat the whole process until we had a platter full of wonderful, golden-brown dough cakes. She would bring the platter to the table and we would "dive in"! They were so good. I made dough cakes for my sons while they were growing up, as well as for my grandchildren. My granddaughter, Kasey, carries on this tradition, as her mother, Vicky, did before her. She will make dough cakes for her family's breakfast on special occasions… much to the pleasure of her brother and her dad. Occasionally, I will have family over for breakfast or "brunch" and serve dough cakes. Of course, although I would like to, I no longer fry them in bacon grease, but use hot oil instead. They are still a favorite to all… including me.

All of the food that was possible to be used, was used. I loved (and still do) kidney stew. I know that to most that brings an "ugh" to mind, but it was one of my favorites. My mother loved kidneys too, and occasionally, I would come home from school, and sitting on the back of the stove, keeping warm, would be a small dish of stewed kidneys and onions. She would have made some for her lunch, and knowing that I loved them, she would save a bit for me to have when I came home. That was, to me, a snack far better than sweets.

I don't have stewed kidneys very often any more. Number one, I never see them in the market and number two, organ meats are supposed to clog up my arteries. I would take that risk though, if I could find them… just to "pig out" once in a while on what is still one of my favorite comfort foods.

Rather like playing the piano, I cook, not because I need to, but because it gives me great satisfaction. I cook when I am happy, I cook when I feel sad, upset, or sometimes, just because I love to.

Thanks, Mom.

EPILOGUE

And so, you have read these vignettes of my early years, when I was growing up in Townsend Harbor. I have hundreds more stories, but I have tried to be a bit selective… not an easy task.

The work ethic has stayed with me, as have many or most of the teachings of my parents. Sometimes, when my own family was growing up, I would hear my father's or mother's words coming out of my mouth: "If you're going to fight, go out in the yard and do it," or "Don't depend on anyone but yourself," and "I don't care if everybody else is going… you're not everybody else." Those are a few among many. I have even added a few of my own, such as, " You don't have to like me… this is not a popularity contest," and, "Pretty is as pretty does."

The openness of our home was, and still is, pretty much the same as my parents': "Our door is always open" to friends and friends of friends, whether they are eight or eighty. As I was growing up, not a lot of people knocked at our door… most just walked in. One of my father's favorite sayings was, "Come anytime! The door is always open!" And it was! And they did!

It was a shock to my husband, Fred, the first time he came to our door. We had, for quite a few months, been "unofficially" dating. I was barely 15 years old when we met at a basketball game. (That is one of my favorite stories to be told… perhaps, some other time.) Fred was nearly 17. I was not allowed to date until I was 16, so Fred would occasionally come to Townsend with his buddies, and we would "meet" at a basketball game or at band concerts on Thursday nights. Sometimes, he would come to town for a school dance. It was not easy for him to get to Townsend, however, because it was 21 miles from Westford (his home town) to Townsend. He did not have a car, so he relied on his pals to help out with the nurturing of this new romance. (If no pal was available, he would, at times, hitchhike to Townsend.) By this time we had a telephone, but it was a toll call from his house to mine, so phone calls were few and far between. We relied on the good old postal service and would exchange letters almost weekly. (I still have those letters.)

When I turned sixteen, we had our first "come and pick me up" date. It was in October of 1949, and he had been allowed to borrow his father's car.

I was upstairs getting ready when he knocked on the door… the one everyone used. My father and my brother Larry were in the kitchen and my mom was in the living room. Fred heard a voice call, "Come in; it's open." Now, Fred had not grown up in a family that was as relaxed and informal as mine was. He was not sure if he should actually walk into a strange house or not. He decided "not" and knocked again. This time the response was a bit louder, "Wear out your knuckles or come in. The door is open."

Fred gently opened the door halfway, poked his head in, and rather meekly asked, "Is Alice here?" (not being sure how he was going to be received). Brother Larry, who could seldom resist a new target for teasing, answered, "No. She's out on a date with some guy. You must have the wrong night. I'm her brother Larry."

I had come downstairs and just then, came into the kitchen to find poor 17-year-old Fred trying to deal with this situation. At that point, he was probably thinking that maybe he would just go home and never have to see these people (including the little blonde) again. He looked very relieved at seeing me there!

I grabbed my coat. As soon as I had introduced him to all, I got him out of there... being thankful that there was only one sibling home that night rather than his having to deal with the larger crew. I think in years to come, he, too, realized how lucky he was to have been able to meet them gradually, as opposed to having had to be inundated with the unusual Conner sense of humor multiplied by 10.

I hurried out the door with him that night. When the date had ended, and I had come back through that door, at 16 years old, I knew I was in love. That night eventually led to a happy and productive marriage that lasted for 46 years, until death parted us.

Yes, the same door that Pat had knocked on to tease Charlotte, the insurance man had knocked on only to be met by a wet mop, and the door Fred had knocked on to pick me up for our first "real" date, probably had been opened and closed nearly a million times in my 18 years in that house.

Through that old door, Mickey had emerged, at one minute before seven every weekday morning. Many babies had been carried through (though I was the first newborn in our family to cross the threshold, because all of the others had been born before my parents moved into that house). Four sons had left for the Army or Navy, and seven daughters had gone off on their first dates through that door. Each girl had passed through for the last time as a single girl, and had returned as a married woman. The sons had come back through that door, returning home on leave from military service. Two of them, during WWII, had happily passed back through that door and returned to the safety and warmth of Mom's kitchen... hopefully closing out some of the horrors of war they had experienced.

Amazing, when you think of it, how much our lives are influenced by simply passing through a door. I think of it now... if they had never brought that old piano through that door... or if I had never walked out that door to go on that first date with Fred....

ABOUT THE AUTHOR

Jean Sutter and Judy Axtell

Alice Conner Selfridge grew up in a small town in rural Massachusetts. She refers to herself as a "late bloomer," not attending college and receiving her degree until her children were all in school, and not publishing this, her first book, until the age of 79.

Alice…author, poet, and storyteller, has a gift for bringing the readers and/or listeners into her world.

Through the family dynamics described in her book, it is apparent how her parents and siblings have influenced her. She cherishes the legacy and traditions that have been passed to her, and she has, in turn, passed on to her family.

Alice is the mother of four boys and is "Lil' Nana" to her eight grandchildren and six great-grandchildren.

In addition to raising her family, she worked at and enjoyed a variety of careers. After becoming a Registered Nurse, she worked as charge nurse in a geriatric facility, and later in a crisis intervention unit. She performed nursing duties, and supervised and taught aides in the home health care industry. She moved to Vermont with her husband Fred, where she taught health and home skills at a private residential school for teenagers with special needs. Mixed in with her busy schedules, she enjoyed producing variety shows (at local schools), quilting, sewing, and was a partner in a wallpapering business.

Alice's family has been steeped in tradition. From her love of the "home-spun," her children and their children have learned to appreciate her pickles and pies, her music, her yearly Christmas poem, and most of all her traditional family values, her wisdom, and her ever-present humor. Family is everything to her!

Alice now resides in Montgomery, New York with her rescued dog, "Maggie".

CPSIA information can be obtained
at www.ICGtesting.com
Printed in the USA
BVHW040303180920
588825BV00021B/269

9 781478 720713